1,818
Ways to
Write Better
& Get
Published

About the Author

Scott Edelstein is the author of several books for writers: *Manuscript Submission* (Writer's Digest Books), *30 Steps to Becoming a Writer—and Getting Published* (Writer's Digest Books), *The Indispensable Writer's Guide* (HarperCollins) and *The No-Experience-Necessary Writer's Course* (Scarborough House). He has published over a hundred short pieces in a variety of publications, ranging from *Writer's Yearbook* to *Glamour* to *Essence* to *A Beginner's Guide to Getting Published*. He is also the author of three books on higher education.

Scott has been a successful freelance writer and editor since 1978. He has also worked as a writing consultant, journalist, staff writer, ghostwriter, literary agent, and a book, magazine, and newspaper editor. He has taught many forms of writing (fiction, nonfiction, poetry, science fiction/fantasy, writing for publication, business writing, technical writing, and composition) at several colleges and universities, as well as through writers' centers, community centers, and other institutions.

He lives in Minneapolis, where he continues to write, edit and consult.

1,818
Ways to
Write Better
& Get
Published

Scott Edelstein

WRITER'S DIGEST BOOKS
CINCINNATI, OH

1,818 Ways to Write Better & Get Published. Copyright © 1991 by Scott Edelstein. Printed and bound in the United States of America. All rights reserved. No part of this book may be reproduced in any form or by any electronic or mechanical means including information storage and retrieval systems without permission in writing from the publisher, except by a reviewer, who may quote brief passages in a review. Published by Writer's Digest Books, an imprint of F&W Publications, Inc., 1507 Dana Avenue, Cincinnati, Ohio 45207. (800) 289-0963. First edition. First paperback printing 1997. This book has been previously published as *The Writer's Book of Checklists* and has been updated.

Other fine Writer's Digest Books are available from your local bookstore or direct from the publisher.

01   00   99   98   97   6   5   4   3   2

Library of Congress Cataloging-in-Publication Data

Edelstein, Scott.
    1,818 ways to write better & get published : the quick-reference guide to essential information every writer needs / by Scott Edelstein.—1st ed.
        p.   cm.
    ISBN 0-89879-778-0
    1. Authorship.   I. Title.
    PN151.E3   1991
    808'.02—dc20   90-28097
                                                                              CIP

Edited by Nan Dibble
Designed by Carol Buchanan

Contents

Introduction
How This Book Is Different

1,818 Ways to Write Better & Get Published provides vital, thorough, up-to-date information on a wide range of writing and publishing topics. It's intended as a basic reference tool for writers (and aspiring writers) of all types. Writers of fiction and nonfiction will find it especially useful.

What sets this book apart from all others on writing is the way it's written. It's made up entirely of checklists. Information on each topic is presented in a clear, concise, easy-to-follow list of key points and principles, usually no longer than six hundred words, and often much briefer. The book's organizing principles are speed and straightforwardness. You can locate and absorb the information you need on over a hundred writing topics with maximum speed and efficiency, and a minimum of searching. In short, this comprehensive yet concise reference book will not only inform you, but will save you time and trouble.

Readers unfamiliar with my previous books for writers may want to know what qualifies me to write this volume. I've been a professional writer for nearly twenty years, with nine published books and over a hundred published stories and articles to my credit. Some of my previous books for writers include *The Indispensable Writer's Guide* (HarperCollins), *The No-Experience-Necessary Writer's Course* (Scarborough House), and *Manuscript Submission* (Writer's Digest Books). I've taught writing at several colleges and universities, and I've worked as a journalist, staff writer, writing consultant, literary agent, ghostwriter, and as a book, magazine, and newspaper editor. I've written this book so that you can easily, quickly, and directly benefit from my experience.

1,818 Ways to Write Better & Get Published is the handiest, easiest-to-use resource guide for writers you can buy. Keep it on your desk, next to your dictionary, ready to use whenever you have a question or need information.

1
The Writer's Attitude

Good and Bad Reasons to Be a Writer

Good Reasons

1. To communicate to others your ideas, emotions, experiences, cares, needs, concerns, questions, and obsessions.
2. To express yourself and who you are.
3. To make money.
4. For personal satisfaction and pleasure.
5. To give satisfaction and pleasure to others.
6. To grow emotionally, intellectually, psychologically, artistically, and/or spiritually; to help others to do the same.
7. To see your name in print.
8. To help establish your reputation, authority, or expertise in a subject, and/or to build your career.
9. For self-knowledge; to better understand and get in touch with yourself.
10. To provide catharsis — to enable what's inside of you to come out.
11. To play with words, concepts, images, and meanings.
12. To persuade others to do, believe, or feel what you would like them to do, believe, or feel.
13. To move others.
14. To move yourself.
15. To develop your thinking, writing, and general communication skills.
16. To help yourself stay (or become) stable, grounded, and happy.
17. To give life to the images, ideas, voices, fantasies, hopes, fears, and/or goals inside you.
18. To escape from normal day-to-day reality — and/or to enable readers to do the same.
19. To pass time pleasurably.
20. To entertain yourself and/or others.
21. To improve your life, and/or the lives of your readers.
22. To earn prestige, admiration, approval, or appreciation from others.
23. To impress others and/or yourself with your literary skill.
24. To create, or attempt to create, great art.
25. To leave your mark on the world.
26. To offer something meaningful to others.

27. To inform or educate others.
28. To tell the truth about something, particularly if the truth is not widely known or accepted.
29. To create something to give or pass on to your loved ones.
30. To provide a written record of important thoughts, feelings, or incidents in your life.
31. To have fun.

Bad Reasons
1. To hurt other people or take revenge on them.
2. To libel or defame others.
3. To feel superior to others or make others feel small.
4. To defraud others.
5. To make, or attempt to make, other people miserable, envious, or unhappy.
6. To make yourself miserable. (If writing makes you miserable, don't be a writer!)
7. To avoid working, supporting your family, or fulfilling any other responsibility.
8. To impress others with the fact that you're a writer.
9. To more readily hang around and be accepted by writers, editors, and other literary types.
10. For the (alleged) increased sex appeal and/or glamour—both of which consistently elude 99 percent of all writers.

24 Common Misconceptions About Writers and Writing

The following notions are widely accepted, but each is largely or entirely false. Statements that begin "Writers are" may in fact be true for some *writers, but by no means for all of them.*

1. A writer must suffer.
2. Writers must reach deep (or as deeply as possible) into their souls when they write.
3. Writers are cerebral, intellectual people—maybe even eggheads.
4. Writing is a noble act.
5. Writers are wise.
6. Writers are unhappy.

7. Writers are dreamers or philosophers at heart.
8. Writing is not a "real job" like accounting or selling cars.
9. Getting published is easy.
10. Getting published is nearly impossible unless you know the right people.
11. Anyone can write a bestseller.
12. You have to live in or near New York City (or Toronto, or Los Angeles) to succeed as a writer.
13. You must "pay your dues" to become a successful writer — usually by enduring years of rejection, emotional pain, and/ or poverty.
14. You must give up everything else to be a writer.
15. If you are serious about writing, you must make it your number one priority.
16. You're not a real writer unless you've written for _____ years (or published _____ books, or written _____ words).
17. You must write every day (or for a certain length of time, or at the same time each day).
18. The only good reason to write is to make money.
19. Making money is not a good reason to write.
20. You must have a room (or other area) of your own just for writing.
21. You must be completely free from distraction and interruption to write well.
22. A writer has to have the latest in writing technology (or a particular piece of equipment) to really write well.
23. You must bare your soul in everything you write.
24. All writers are a little bit (or more than a little bit) crazy.

The 10 Biggest Writing Fears—and How to Get Over Them

The Fears
1. I don't have any (or enough) talent.
2. I don't know how to say what I want to say. (Or, I don't know how to write anything creative.)
3. I don't know where or how to start.
4. I don't know what I want to say. (Or, I don't have anything to say.)
5. I can get started, but then I get stuck.

6. I might hate writing.
7. What I write might turn out awful, or I might not be able to finish it at all.
8. I might be wasting my time.
9. I'll never be as good as Grace Paley, or Alice Walker, or the man with the mustache in my writers' group.
10. People might say critical or nasty things about what I've written.

How to Get Over Them
1. Write.
2. When fears arise, acknowledge them *and keep writing anyway*.
3. If any of your fears turns out to be true, admit to yourself that it's true — at least for the moment — *and keep writing*.
4. Continue writing as well as you can. As time passes, your fears will have less and less power over you.

23 Tools of the Writer's Trade

Absolutely Essential
1. Your choice of writing materials: pens, sharp pencils, a typewriter, a computer, or a word processor.
2. Plenty of paper. Use white unlined bond (16- or 20-pound; photocopy paper is excellent) for final drafts and letters, whatever you like for notes and earlier drafts.
3. Correction fluid (such as Wite-Out or Liquid Paper).
4. A good, thick dictionary — preferably unabridged. Webster's Second Edition is ideal.

Extremely Important
5. File folders; a place to keep them (a filing cabinet or cardboard box); a system for keeping track of them.
6. Scissors.
7. Transparent tape.
8. A 12-inch ruler.
9. Plain white (#10) business envelopes.
10. Large (9″ × 12″ or 10″ × 13″) clasp envelopes.
11. Erasers (both ink and pencil).
12. Paper clips (both regular and jumbo).

13. A pencil sharpener.
14. A good, thick thesaurus — one that's alphabetical, not one that's arranged by subject.

Highly Recommended

15. Butterfly clamps (large paper clips in a butterfly shape).
16. A sturdy stapler and spare staples.
17. Rubber bands.
18. Correction tape (adhesive white tape for covering and correcting errors).
19. Blank mailing labels (approximately 1" × 3").
20. Spare typewriter or printer ribbons, correction ribbons, computer disks, daisy wheels, etc.
21. The current edition of *Writer's Market* or *Novel and Short Story Writer's Market*, *Poet's Market*, *Children's Writer's & Illustrator's Market*, etc.
22. A submission book (for keeping track of which editors have which manuscripts — see pages 168-169 for details).
23. A postage scale (for weighing submissions and other small packages).

Setting Up Your Workspace

Whether it's a plush office or a corner of your kitchen, you want the place(s) where you write to be as comfortable and as supportive of your efforts as a writer as possible. Here are some things to consider:

1. Do you write best with a computer terminal, dedicated word processor, typewriter, pen, or pencil? What color ink or ribbon works best for you? What type size (10, 12, or 15 pitch) and typeface do you like the most? What style, color, and size of paper do you prefer? Buy whatever tools, brands, styles, and colors most please you — after all, you're the one doing the writing.
2. Is everything you need for writing close at hand and easy to reach? Arrange pens, paper, envelopes, and other supplies so that you don't have to get up to fetch something.
3. Is there enough room for you to work comfortably?

4. Are your chair and your writing surface the right height? Two or three inches can make a big difference in comfort and, potentially, in your creativity or productivity.
5. Is the lighting adequate and appropriate? Light that's too low or too harsh can cause eyestrain and fatigue. Do you prefer natural, incandescent, or fluorescent light? Do you work better with the whole room lit, or with a tight beam focused on your work area?
6. How much privacy do you require? Do you need a whole room with a door that you can close? An area separate from the rest of the house? Do you need a "Do Not Disturb" sign?
7. What about noise? Can you write with background noise, or do you need quiet? Will a phone in your office be pleasantly accessible or a source of interruption? Do you want to be able to play music while you write?
8. Consider temperature and humidity. Do you need a fan, a portable heater, or a humidifier?
9. What sort of view would you like as you work? The garden outside? A blank wall? A full bookshelf? Your own reflection?
10. What other things can you provide to make yourself as comfortable, creative, and productive as possible? A coffee maker? A cooler of iced tea? A windup toy to tinker with? Pictures of your kids?
11. Most important of all, what is the overall effect of your workspace? Is it a spot where you feel good—and a place where you feel like writing?
12. When you run low on anything (paper, typewriter ribbons, or other supplies), replenish your stock before it's all gone. It's disturbing to run out of an important item while you're writing.
13. Not everyone works best at a desk. If you're most comfortable writing in bed, or perched in a tree, or sitting in a coffee shop, make that your regular workplace.
14. Your clothing is a part of your work environment. Wear clothes that keep you adequately warm or cool, and that you feel comfortable writing in.

Finding the Best Times to Write

1. Observe yourself when you write. What length of time constitutes an ideal "writing stint" for you? Two hours? Four hours? Two forty-five minute periods with a half-hour break in between?
2. Look at your own mental, physical, and emotional cycles. When are you most alert, creative, and imaginative? Early in the morning? Late at night? Just after supper?
3. Note those times when you have the fewest distractions and demands. Is this during your lunch hour? After your family has gone to bed? On Sunday afternoons?
4. Look at the times that appear in *both* your responses to item 2 *and* your response to item 3. These are your ideal writing times.
5. Pick from among these times. Because your writing time is important to you, put these times on your calendar, so that you don't ignore or forget about them. Schedule your writing time in comfortable, productive blocks, according to your response to item 1 above.
6. If there is no overlap between the times in your list for item 2 and those in your list for item 3, pick at least one block of time from *each* of the two lists.
7. When the time for writing arrives, use it for writing—not for anything else.

14 Principles of Etiquette for Writers

1. Use proper manuscript form.
2. Accompany all submissions with cover letters, typed in a standard business letter format.
3. Use standard written American English except in special circumstances (as in dialogue). You do not normally need to follow the rules of a particular style manual. (Exceptions: some scholarly, professional, and technical journals.)
4. Whenever you quote another person, or substantially borrow information or ideas, be sure to cite your source.
5. Never claim anyone else's words or ideas as your own.

6. Don't lie, twist the truth, or make up information or details in any piece intended to be factual.
7. Present your credentials truthfully and accurately, but in the most positive, truthful light you can.
8. Never promise something you can't deliver.
9. Be civil and businesslike at all times, whether in letters, in person, or on the phone.
10. Don't be afraid to use the phone, but use it only when a letter will be less efficient, convenient, or useful. Call collect only when you have been specifically asked to call.
11. Abide by the terms of all agreements you make. Expect editors and other publishing people to do the same.
12. Never agree to any terms you are unwilling or unable to meet.
13. If a problem arises, make it known to the appropriate people promptly and straightforwardly.
14. Don't threaten a lawsuit unless your other options for solving the problem have been exhausted. Don't file a lawsuit unless the threat doesn't work.

How to Live With Rejection

1. Always remember that only the piece you submitted has been rejected—*not* you as a person or a writer.
2. Never forget that getting rejected is a natural part of being a writer. Virtually every writer on the planet, no matter how talented, successful, or well known, has had work rejected, often repeatedly.
3. Remind yourself that pieces get rejected all the time for all kinds of reasons, some of them having nothing to do with the pieces themselves. Just because an editor says no doesn't mean that your piece isn't well done or worth reading and publishing.
4. Don't let rejection shake your faith in a piece, or in your writing ability in general. If you believe in something, keep submitting it.
5. Be patient. Don't expect to get your first or second piece accepted for publication. Your fifteenth or twentieth is a more reasonable goal.
6. Persevere. You may have to submit something ten, twenty,

or even fifty times before an editor says yes to it.

7. Encourage yourself by reminding yourself regularly of your skills and achievements as a writer.

8. If you've received any of the following, put them in a prominent place (e.g., above your desk), so that they will regularly affirm your writing goals and ability: letters from editors accepting your work, rejection letters that praise your work or your writing ability, photocopies of publishers' checks, and/or copies of your publications.

9. When a piece is rejected, don't let it gather dust. Send it to another editor promptly.

10. Keep several (or more than several) copies of each piece in circulation at once. This maximizes your chances for success.

11. Counter the emotional sting of rejection by doing something you enjoy — seeing a movie, going out for an Italian dinner, walking through the park — every time (or every fifth time) one of your pieces is rejected.

12. If you get thoroughly sick and tired of rejection, put up a sign above your desk that says, "Some editors wouldn't know good writing if it bit them on the butt." If your symptoms persist, add an illustration.

13. Remind yourself that advancement in any career or endeavor takes time, energy, patience, and persistence.

14. Don't get discouraged. Recall that *Gone with the Wind* was rejected over fifteen times, and *Zen and the Art of Motorcycle Maintenance* over a hundred, before a publisher finally said yes.

15. *Never* write or call editors to argue the merits of a rejected piece, to tell them how foolish or short-sighted they are, or to ask for critiques or why they said no. You'll only alienate them. Accept each rejection philosophically and move on.

16. Never tell an editor in a cover letter that the piece you're submitting has been rejected already. Let the editor make a fresh judgment.

17. If a department editor at a magazine or newspaper turns your piece down, try it on an editor in a different department *at that same publication*. For example, if the feature editor at a newspaper says no, perhaps the lifestyles editor or the Sunday supplement editor will say yes. (Your

piece must, of course, be appropriate for whatever department(s) you approach.)

18. If an editor rejects your piece, and that editor is later replaced, try the same piece on their replacement.
19. If an editor likes your piece, but not quite enough to take it, feel free to rewrite it and submit the rewrite, even if the editor did not ask or invite you to.
20. *Never* throw a piece away, no matter how many times it has been rejected. What is unpublishable today may be very publishable a year (or ten years) from now.
21. Keep writing as well as you can. The most effective cure for the Rejection Blues is to be the very best writer you can be.

How to Live With Success

1. When success (however you may define it) comes, don't assume that it will continue indefinitely — or even for the next six months. What is hot today may be of little interest to readers or editors half a year from now.
2. Keep in mind that no matter what happens, your career will have both ups and downs for as long as you continue writing.
3. *Never* assume that a great flow of money will continue. Pay any federal, state, and local estimated taxes on your writing income immediately; then save or invest much of what remains.
4. Never spend — or count on — any money from any publisher until you have received a check and deposited it, *and it has cleared.*
5. Don't make any sudden or potentially disruptive changes in your lifestyle. Before you do make any major change, be sure that you, those close to you, and your finances can all handle it.
6. Avoid thinking that your success means you are a better writer than someone with less fame or money. It does take talent to succeed, but for every talented person who achieves much, there are two or three equally talented people whose success is far more modest.
7. *Never* use your success to act — or feel — superior to others.

Gloating is bad for both your conscience and your reputation.

8. Don't rest on your laurels. The best way to continue your success is to keep writing and sending out your work.
9. When negotiating future publication agreements, use your past success to negotiate for more money and better terms.
10. Continue to support and build your writing career by doing book signings, appearing on TV and radio talk shows, granting media interviews, going on a speaking or reading tour, etc.
11. Help other good writers to attain success by writing endorsements, recommendations or introductions for their works.
12. Keep growing as a writer.
13. Be grateful for your success.
14. Enjoy yourself.

Responding to Comments, Criticism, and Reviews

1. Always remember that the final judgment on anything you've written is yours and yours alone.
2. Consider each comment or suggestion carefully, on its own merits — regardless of who or where it came from. If it makes sense, follow it; if it doesn't, ignore it.
3. Remember that the same person can be absolutely right about certain aspects of a piece and dead wrong about others.
4. Never take any criticism of your work personally. Your piece is being criticized, not you. People who criticize you on the basis of your work are being both rude and foolish.
5. No matter how certain some people may be about their views, and no matter how hard they may push you to accept them, you *never* have to do or agree with what they say.
6. When seeking criticism, try to get feedback from at least two different people. Ideally, these should be people you trust, as well as the kind of readers your piece is meant to reach.
7. Keep in mind that some people's comments or reviews may be downright daft. Don't take bizarre criticism *or* bizarre praise seriously.

8. *Never* write to a publication that has reviewed your work to argue with, criticize, or complain about the reviewer; this only makes you look petty and childish. You may, however, write to correct any factual errors in the review.
9. Try not to get angry, no matter what anyone says about your work. If your critic is wrong, getting angry won't do you any good; if they're right, there's nothing to get angry about.
10. Keep in mind that nothing you write will ever please everyone; there will always be someone ready with a "thumbs down." *Romeo and Juliet* and *Moby Dick* both received some scathing reviews from prominent critics.

Spotting and Ignoring Bad Advice

How to Spot Bad Advice
1. Any idea or suggestion that is presented as universal ("all poems must," "all mysteries have to," "all writers must," "all good stories always," etc.) is at least highly suspect, if not wholly false.
2. Ignore any appeal to authority ("The editor at the *Ohio Review* feels exactly the same way," or "Professor Gosset at Princeton thought it was first-rate"). Accept suggestions and criticism on their own merits, not because of who or where they come from.
3. Be wary of appeals to consensus (for example, "The whole class agrees that the scene in the steel mill needs rewriting.") Again, consider comments and ideas entirely on their own merits.
4. Be suspicious of people who, when offering suggestions or criticism, compliment themselves or their own work.
5. Anything vague, unclear, or ambiguous can do more harm than good. Ask for clarification.
6. Listen to your gut. If what somebody says feels and sounds wrong, it probably is. If it feels and sounds right, however, it's worth trying.

How to Ignore Bad Advice
1. Listen politely.
2. Thank people for their suggestions.

3. Once you're alone with your piece, do what you believe is best.

10 Reasons to Be Persistent and Patient

These reasons apply to writing a particular piece, to waiting for editors and agents to respond to your work, and to building a writing career.

1. You have to be. It's a necessary part of being a writer.
2. Being patient and persistent works. The people who make it as writers are those who have practiced patience and persistence for years.
3. It's saner, more comfortable, and less stressful than being impatient and giving up.
4. Decisions, pieces of writing, and careers all need time to grow, mature, and ripen.
5. Editors, agents, and other publishing people are often overwhelmingly busy, and thus slow to respond to writers.
6. Quick success is extremely rare, both in writing and in all other fields. Most writers succeed only as the result of much effort, time, and perseverance.
7. Patience and persistence will do more to get you through the inevitable ups and downs of being a writer than anything else.
8. The less energy you spend anticipating and worrying, the more you'll have to put into your writing and into building your writing career.
9. If anyone tells you that you have no talent, that you're wasting your time, or that you'll never make it as a writer, you'll be able to simply smile and continue writing.
10. No one else can be persistent and patient for you.

2
The Writer's Craft

▸

▸

▸

Keeping a Journal or Notebook

Your journal will be yours alone, so begin by looking for the ideal blank book: one that you feel most comfortable with, and that has the dimensions and features you desire.

Selecting a Blank Book for Your Journal

1. First, browse through bookstores, office supply stores, gift shops, and stationery stores to discover the wide range of options available.
2. Consider the size and shape that will best suit you. You want a book that's easy to carry with you. Think about whether you will be carrying it in your pocket, purse, or briefcase.
3. Ask yourself if you want to be able to tear pages out of your notebook.
4. Think about whether you want to be able to rearrange the pages.
5. Consider the overall feel of your notebook. Do you want something visually attractive and artsy, or no-nonsense and businesslike? Which emphasis does more to inspire you to write?
6. Think about the cover of your notebook. What color do you prefer? Should it be very sturdy, like a hardbound book, or will something more inexpensive do? Do you want an illustration or design of any kind?
7. Ask yourself whether you prefer writing on small pages (e.g., $6'' \times 9''$) or large ones (e.g., $8\frac{1}{2}'' \times 11''$)?
8. Consider whether you prefer lined or unlined paper. If you prefer lines, do you like them close together or farther apart?
9. Think about what you're willing to spend. Small spiral-bound notebooks sell for under a dollar; handmade blank books can cost as much as twenty.
10. Using your responses to the above questions, make a list of all the qualities you want in a blank book (for example, bound pages, large size, sturdy cover in plain black, etc.). Then go hunting for exactly what best suits you.

Some Options for Journals
1. Handmade blank books.
2. Mass-produced blank books.
3. Writers' journals: blank books with pertinent quotations on each page (e.g., *A Woman's Journal*).
4. Spiral-bound notebooks.
5. Two- and three-ring binders.
6. Legal pads.

Preparing Your Journal
1. Write your name, address, and phone number(s) in indelible ink in an easy-to-see spot, such as the inside front cover.
2. Attach one — or better, two — writing implements directly to your journal, so that you are never without something to write with. This can be as simple as closing a pencil inside the book, or slipping the pocket-grip of a pen onto one of the pages.
3. If you like, decorate the cover or attach something inspiring (such as a photo of May Sarton or a photocopy of a publisher's check) to it.
4. Carry your journal with you wherever you go, so that it is always ready to use, and so that you get used to picking it up whenever you leave your home. Or if, like me, you worry about losing your journal, keep it in a safe place at home. When you go out, always take paper and a pencil or pen with you. Use these to write down whatever you wish; then, when you get home, transfer your notes to your journal.
5. As part of your bedtime routine, put your journal next to your bed, so that you can write down any important insights, images, or dreams that come to you during the night.

Making the Best Use of Your Journal
1. Write down ideas, images, and observations in your journal as soon as possible after they come to you, so that none of them slip through the cracks of your memory.
2. Spend a few minutes with your journal when you wake up in the morning, and again toward the end of the day, so that you can mentally review the past hours and write down anything important that you may have overlooked.
3. If you like, separate your journal into sections — one for

ideas for pieces, another for pertinent observations, another for character sketches, another for first drafts of poems, etc. Or, if you prefer, keep a separate section for each piece you're working on.

4. Keep your eyes, ears, and other senses open for anything worth writing down, such as bits of overheard conversation, intriguing facts, or unexpected observations.

5. Periodically "mine" your journal: look through it for lines, ideas, images, and early drafts that you can use in pieces you're working on.

Locating Material for Your Work

1. Above all, keep your eyes, ears, and other senses open. The more you let in, the more material (and the more sources of material) you will find.

2. Try new things. Experiment. Search for, do, and experience things you've never done or experienced before. New experience is one of the best sources of inspiration — plus, the more you've done, the more you have to write about.

3. If there's something you can't or won't do, *pretend* you did it. Write about what might have happened. Don't be afraid to fake it.

4. Let your imagination go. Deliberately fantasize. Follow your hunches and intuition.

5. Experiment with what you write. Try new approaches, forms, genres, styles, and voices. Stretch your range. Play.

6. Use your dreams, daydreams, and fantasies. Write down the most powerful of these in your journal. If you like, keep a log of your dreams.

7. Ask yourself what you really care about. What thrills, infuriates, astounds, terrifies, excites, shocks, disturbs, or deeply embarrasses you? The more strongly or deeply you respond to something, the more it means to you, and the more you are likely to have to say about it.

8. Spend some time recalling those smells, sights, tastes, sounds, and physical sensations that move or mean something to you. Write these down in a list; then work with them.

9. Read. In fact, read a lot — the work of good writers, the work

of not-so-good writers, news magazines, billboards, junk mail, labels on peanut butter jars. It's all grist for your mill.
10. Do research. Don't be afraid to dig for information. Use the library; make phone calls; write letters of inquiry.
11. Talk with people—particularly exotic or unusual people. Get them to tell you about their jobs, their childhoods, or their families. Almost everyone has some fascinating stories to tell, but most of us need some coaxing. Remember to do more listening than talking.

9 Ways to Generate Fresh Ideas

1. Ask yourself, "What if?" For any issue or situation, imagine the best, worst, most unlikely, and most unexpected scenarios.
2. Don't be afraid to be weird, illogical, or extreme. Sometimes outright absurdity is the answer—or will lead you to the answer.
3. Relax for a few minutes, focusing your attention on your piece or your literary problem. Then let your mind wander for half an hour or more, and see where it leads you. Keep pen and paper nearby.
4. Deliberately (but surreptitiously and tactfully) eavesdrop on other people's conversations. This helps generate an astonishing number of ideas and insights.
5. Combine two or three elements that would normally not be combined—a McDonald's on Mars, an alcoholic Care Bear, etc.—to create something unexpected and original.
6. Ask yourself what *you* would most like to read that hasn't been written yet. Then write that piece yourself.
7. Look in unlikely places—the Sydney Yellow Pages, your mother's high school yearbook, a map of the Toronto subway system, etc. Browse through odd and unusual sources.
8. Visit unlikely places, too: a shoelace factory, an abandoned steel mill, the area behind the mechanical pinsetters at a bowling alley, etc.
9. Sit down with one, two, or several people whose minds you respect. Brainstorm. Toss around ideas. Shoot the bull. Argue. Take notes.

Rewriting and Editing Your Work

1. **Rewriting**, revising, and revision all mean the same thing: looking at a piece again and writing it over, using a fresh approach or perspective. The result of each rewrite is a new **draft** of your piece.

2. **Editing** is a very different process from rewriting: it involves making adjustments and smoothing out rough edges in a piece that is basically in good shape. **Polishing** means minor editing.

3. Editing is not just something editors do. You must edit your own work, line by line and word by word, to make sure it is in the best possible shape.

4. **Proofreading** is the process of checking for technical problems such as omitted words, improper punctuation, and misspellings.

5. Editing comes only after revising. If you need to make a major change in your piece (adding a character or incident, changing the viewpoint, etc.), editing won't do the trick; you'll need to revise or add to what you have. Proofreading follows editing and polishing.

6. Remember that all decisions regarding the rewriting of your piece are ultimately your own, no matter what anyone else suggests or says. (In a collaboration, of course, decisions on rewriting are normally made jointly by the coauthors.)

7. Decisions on editing, however, are not always your own. Many publishers request or insist on the right to edit work for publication as they see fit.

8. Keep in mind that there are many different ways to rewrite, and many different legitimate approaches to it. Feel free to do whatever seems best for your piece.

9. There is no "right" number of rewrites for any given piece of writing. Some pieces need dozens of rewrites; some require none. One to three rewrites is common. Do however many revisions are necessary to get your piece into finished shape.

10. Most writers do their best work by letting everything come out onto the page in a rush—unedited, uncensored, and unpolished. Then they go back and reread and rewrite what they've written. Trying to rewrite each phrase and sentence

as it comes out blocks their flow of words.

11. You don't have to rewrite your piece from beginning to end. You can start anywhere, working on one section at a time. Some sections may need several rewrites, others only one, or none at all.

12. When revising, start with the largest concerns (such as plot, point of view, central metaphor, and setting) first. There's no point in worrying about comma placement or a character's name if you need a whole new plot. Once the big things seem right, work on the less crucial concerns (such as dialogue, tone, and pacing). Then concentrate on individual paragraphs or stanzas.

13. Read each draft aloud, listening to each word and phrase. Your ear will catch problems and provide insights that your eye won't.

14. Between drafts or rewrites, put your piece aside for some time — a week, a day, or at least overnight — so that when you reread it you have a fresh and more objective perspective.

15. Some writers like to rewrite without looking at their previous drafts; others prefer revising with one or more of their previous drafts beside them, so that they can reuse good lines, paragraphs, concepts, and images.

16. Watch for diminishing returns as you rewrite. When your piece is basically in good shape, stop rewriting and proceed to the next step, editing. The same principle applies to editing and proofreading. When you have read through your piece twice and made only a few minor changes both times, stop working: the piece is probably finished.

17. If an editor asks you to rewrite your piece, don't automatically say yes or no. Judge each suggestion, criticism, and request on its own merits.

18. When an editor requests a rewrite, you do not have to do everything they ask. Most or all changes are negotiable. Feel free to compromise, offer alternatives, bargain one change for another, ask for an explanation or rationale, or explain your own intentions. It's also okay to refuse to rewrite something. (This might or might not cost you the sale.)

19. If an editor asks you to rewrite and resubmit a piece, they are under no obligation whatsoever to accept your rewrite for publication, even if you followed the editor's suggestions to the letter. (The one exception is a piece written on assignment, then rewritten to the editor's clear specifications.)

20. Once you have significantly rewritten a piece, you may try it again on any editors who rejected the earlier version—preferably those who found some merit in that earlier version. If they are likely to recall the previous version, explain in your cover letter that you've done a thorough rewrite; if they are not likely to remember, don't mention it.

21. If you are sent **page proofs** or **galleys** (text set in type that has not yet been formatted into individual pages), edit and proofread them very carefully, and return them promptly. This is part of your job as a writer.

22. Editing is sometimes—though not always—negotiable. If you receive galleys or page proofs for a piece you've written prior to publication, assume that most or all editing decisions are yours. If you receive neither galleys nor page proofs before publication, however, assume the publisher will edit as it chooses.

23. When negotiating a book contract, insist on a clause requiring your publisher to send you galleys or page proofs. You can ask for such a clause when negotiating a magazine agreement as well, although the chances are only one in three that the publisher will say okay.

Copyediting Marks

Use the following marks, symbols, and notations when making corrections in a typed or computer-printed manuscript—one that has not yet been set in type for publication.

Correction	How to Mark Text
1. Insert a letter or number	big rd dog (with inserted "e" and caret ^)
	in the 190s (with caret ^ and inserted "9")
2. Insert a punctuation mark (when there is space between letters or words)	the way So I took (with inserted period)
	Barbara's book is on the (with inserted apostrophe)
3. Insert a punctuation mark (when there is no space between letters or words)	give me your wishlist (with inserted hyphen =)
	Barbaras book is on the (with inserted apostrophe)
4. Insert a space	a tiny flower vase. (with inserted space mark #)
5. Insert a word or group of words	Is this the right one? (with inserted "right")
	wants to play. (with inserted "learn how to")
6. Insert a superscript number	$e = mc^2$
7. Delete a letter or punctuation mark	going back to (with deletion of "g")
	large blue truck (with deletion of comma)
8. Delete a word or group of words	~~single~~ most absurd
	to ~~accept and~~ understand
9. Delete and close space	at be~~g~~ginning
10. Close space	class room 202 (with close-up mark)
11. Replace a word or number with another	Open the ~~window~~. (with "door")
	only ~~45,000~~ people (with 35,500)
12. Change a letter or punctuation mark:	
Method 1	hardly ~~bleathe~~ the (with "breathe")
Method 2	gone that bothered (with inserted period)
Method 3	a huge autombile (with inserted "o")

Correction	How to Mark Text
13. Spell out a number	more than ~~10~~ ^{ten} types of
14. Change a word to a number	at least ~~ninety~~ ⁹⁰
15. Change to lowercase	your dear /Family
16. Change to uppercase	owned by d̲r. Hanke
17. Transpose letters	the typerwiter keys
18. Transpose words	using new/the shovel
19. Set in italics	copy of <u>Moby Dick</u>
20. Begin new paragraph	later.¶ On Friday,
21. No new paragraph; run text as same paragraph	away from him.⌐ NO ¶ Meanwhile, she
22. Ignore indicated correction; leave text as it was originally	Do you ~~genuinely~~ (STET) want the best money can buy?

If a major change — correcting or cutting an entire line, moving several words to another line, etc. — is required, make the change using one of the following methods:

1. Retype the page with the correction included.
2. Make corrections by placing strips of correction tape over the error, then typing the correct text on the tape.
3. Retype the portion of the page that requires correction. Using scissors, glue or tape, and a photocopy machine, create a new, clean, correct page.

A page with more than five or six small corrections should also be retyped.

Proofreader's Marks

Use the following marks, symbols, and notations when correcting galleys and page proofs. Editors use these same symbols and notations.

Correction	How to Mark Text	What to Put in the Margin
1. Insert a letter or number	big r͜d dog	e
	in the 19͜0s	9
2. Insert a period	the way͜ So I took	⊙
3. Insert a comma	under him͜ but then	⌃
4. Insert a semicolon	this matter͜ however,	;/
5. Insert a colon	only two options͜ run or	:/
6. Insert a hyphen	give me your wish͜list	=
7. Insert an apostrophe	Barbara˅s book is on	˅
8. Insert a dash	do it͜ it was simply	⫟
9. Insert quotation marks	said,˅ No way!˅	˶ / ˶
10. Insert a space	a tiny flower͜vase.	#
11. Insert a word or group of words	Is this the͜ one?	right
	wants to͜ play.	learn how to
12. Insert superscript number	e = mc˅	2

Correction	How to Mark Text	What to Put in the Margin
13. Delete a letter or punctuation mark	going̸back to large̸blue truck	ℒ ℒ
14. Delete a word or group of words	~~single~~ most absurd to ~~accept and~~ understand	ℒ ℒ
15. Delete and close space	at beǵginning	ℒ
16. Close space	class ⌒room 202	⌣
17. Replace a word or number with another	Open the ~~window~~. only ~~45,000~~ people	door 35,500
18. Change a letter or punctuation mark	hardly b̸reathe the gone̸ that bothered	r/∧ ;̂
19. Spell out a number	more than ⑩ types	ten
20. Change a word to a number	at least (ninety)	90
21. Change to uppercase	owned by d̲r̲. Hanke	(cap)
22. Change to lowercase	your dear F̸amily	(lc)
23. Transpose letters	the typeⱳriter keys	(tr)
24. Transpose words	using new⁀the shovel	(tr)
25. Move line or lines	line 2 line 1	(tr)
26. Set in italics	copy of <u>Moby Dick</u>	(ital)
27. Set in boldface type	the truly best car	(bf)
28. Set in regular type	(Do you understand?)	(rom)

Correction	How to Mark Text	What to Put in the Margin

29. Set in small capitals   our <u>special</u> offer   (SC)

30. Begin new paragraph   later.¶On Friday,   ¶

31. No new paragraph; run text as same paragraph   away from him.⌐ NO ¶ ⌐Meanwhile, she   NO ¶

32. Ignore indicated correction; leave text as it was originally   Do you ~~genuinely~~ want the best money can buy?   STET

33. Move left   [until the next   move left

34. Move right   until the next   ]   move right

35. Move up   really don't believe   ⌐ ⌐

36. Move down   really don't believe   ⌐ ⌐

37. Move elsewhere   "No," she said. She scratched her head and turned away. "Not yet, anyway."   (tr)

38. Multiple corrections on one line   ghots imaiges onthe   (tr)/♀/#

20 Often-Misused Writing Terms

1. **Ambiguous**: able to be taken or understood in two or more ways at once. Properly used, ambiguity can add depth or impact to a passage or a piece of writing; unintended ambiguity, however, is usually detrimental. Often misused to mean **confusing** or **unclear**. Anything ambiguous expresses an **ambiguity**.
2. **Blank Verse**: unrhymed poetry written in iambic

pentameter. Often misused to mean **free verse** (see below).

3. **Creative Prose**: prose *other than fiction* that is creative rather than reportorial, and that incorporates some of the elements of fiction (metaphor, imagery, epiphany, etc.). Often misunderstood to mean any **prose** (including fiction) that is creative, or creative writing of any type. The term **creative nonfiction** is synonymous.

4. **Denouement**: the final resolution or untangling of events in a literary work. A denouement typically follows the climax of a piece, although it may sometimes include the climax. Sometimes misused to mean **climax**.

5. **Draft**: a version of a piece of writing that has been written or rewritten from beginning to end (more or less). Some writers incorrectly refer to an edited (or slightly edited) version of a draft as a new draft.

6. **Diction**: word choice. Sometimes confused with **grammar** or **syntax** (see below).

7. **e.g.**: for example. Often confused with **i.e.** (see below).

8. **Epiphany**: a point of awakening or understanding, either for a character, the reader, or both. An epiphany can occur at any point in a literary work. Sometimes confused with **climax**.

9. **Free Verse**: verse written without meter or regular rhyme. However, good free verse does make use of other poetic techniques, such as alliteration, metaphor, and imagery. Sometimes confused with **automatic writing**, which means to write down in a steady, unedited stream whatever comes into your head. Also confused with **blank verse** (see above).

10. **i.e.**: that is. Example: "The book was unsatisfactory—i.e., full of precisely the sort of information Carla didn't need." Often confused with **e.g.** (see above).

11. **Irony**: an occurrence or result that is the opposite of what would be normal, expected, or desired. Example: "The book was eight hundred pages long. It contained no useful information." An irony can also be a figure of speech in which the actual meaning is the opposite of the literal meaning. Example: "Gary's night of intense studying consisted of watching David Letterman and eating pizza." Anything expressing an irony is **ironic**. Often misused to mean an occurrence that is strange, unexpected, paradoxical, awful, or funny.

12. **Lyric:** a short poem that expresses a single emotion, narrated by a single person. Often confused with **lyrical,** which means musical. Lyric is a noun, lyrical an adjective.

13. **Mood:** the overall atmosphere or feeling created by a piece of writing (or a portion thereof). Sometimes confused with **tone,** which refers only to the way a piece sounds. Tone and mood can be quite different; in *Arsenic and Old Lace,* for example, the tone is quite chipper, but the mood is creepy.

14. **Obscure:** little-known, unclear, or hard to follow. Sometimes misused to mean **complex.**

15. **Scan:** to identify the meter in a poem, or to have a regular meter. How a poem scans is called **scansion.** Occasionally confused with **rhyme.**

16. **Scene:** a self-contained portion of a literary work, usually limited to a single location, time, point of view, or event. Sometimes confused with **setting,** which is the location where an event, image, observation, or entire piece of writing takes place.

17. **Stream of Consciousness:** a literary technique in which the viewpoint is from inside a character's head. Stream of consciousness may use standard English, as in Nicholson Baker's *The Mezzanine,* or a modified form of English meant to simulate thoughts (as in some of William Faulkner's work). Often confused with **automatic writing** (see above).

18. **Syntax:** sentence structure. Sometimes confused with **grammar, usage,** and **diction** (see above).

19. **Tone:** the way a piece of writing sounds, when read either silently or aloud. Sometimes confused with **mood** (see above).

20. **Viewpoint:** the character through whose eyes an image, scene, or event is viewed. Also called **point of view.** The **viewpoint character** is sometimes confused with the **narrator,** the person or character telling the story. The narrator and viewpoint character are often the same, but they can also be two different people, as in this example: "So there I am, stuck at home, while Karen is out having the time of her life. She begins thinking, 'What's the problem? I like it here,' and she decides right away to scrap her plans to move."

Avoiding Sexism in Your Writing

1. When writing about a hypothetical person, don't say "he," "him," or "his." Instead, use "they," "them," and "their" — or, if you prefer, "he or she," "him or her," and "his or her(s)." If you like, you may reverse the order to "she or he," "her or him," etc. In some cases, it may be possible to rewrite the sentence so as to eliminate pronouns entirely. For example, instead of "They would probably catch the flu," you might write, "The likely outcome: a case of the flu."
2. Avoid the use of "one" (as in, "When one encounters a lion, one wonders whether to freeze or run away"), which has fallen into disuse and disfavor.
3. Sometimes making the reader the hypothetical subject works well, as in, "If you were a judge, you'd want to wear Bermuda shorts under your robes in the summer."
4. Another option is to alternate: use feminine pronouns in one chapter or example, masculine pronouns in the next, and so on.
5. When referring to a specific person whose sex or identity you don't know (e.g., the head of the department of history, the next president of the United States, or the child you plan to have in three years), follow the guidelines in items 1 and 2 above. However, if you do know the person's sex, use the appropriate masculine or feminine pronoun(s).
6. Use "humankind" or "humanity" instead of "mankind"; use "people," "human beings," or "men and women" instead of "men." However, do use "men" to refer to all-male groups (such as the men who served in Lincoln's cabinet), and use "women" for all-female groups (such as the Sisters of St. Catherine).
7. Use words such as "chairperson," "spokesperson," and "salesperson" instead of "chairman," "spokesman," and "salesman" when referring to a hypothetical person or a person whose sex or identity you don't know. Do, however, use "chairman," "spokesman," etc., when you know the person is male — and "spokeswoman," "saleswoman," etc., when you know the person is female.
8. Remember that with extremely few exceptions (such as nuns and professional football players), every profession includes

members of both sexes. There are female ministers and corporate raiders, and male nurses, secretaries, and kindergarten teachers.

9. Clarity is essential in virtually every piece of writing. If in a certain passage, using nonsexist language makes the passage hard to follow or confusing, try to find a different nonsexist way to express it. If you absolutely *must* choose between clarity and sexual equality, choose clarity.

10. Whatever method you choose for achieving sexual equality in your writing, stick with it from the beginning of your piece to the end. Using two or more different approaches may confuse or distract your reader.

11. Each publisher, publication, and style manual has its own way of handling the issue of sexual equality in language. Once a publisher agrees to publish something you've written, it will edit your piece according to its own standard style and policy on nonsexist language. In rare cases (some scholarly, professional, and technical journals), the publisher will specify a particular style manual for you to follow.

16 Ways to Break Writer's Block

Writer's block has many different causes, and an even wider range of solutions. The following strategies have all proven successful for some writers.

1. First, check for external pressures: physical or emotional stress, illness, poor diet, inadequate sleep, excessive distraction, or changes or disruptions in your routine. Fix or eliminate these external factors as much as you can.

2. If a block persists, make a list of all possible directions in which your piece can go. Don't exclude any ideas, even silly or seemingly unworkable ones. Try out one or more of these directions until something clicks.

3. Change where, when, or how you write. Use a pen and paper instead of a computer, or write in the early morning instead of at night.

4. Make your writing circumstances as pleasant and comfortable as possible. Use more (or less) light. Keep a

coffee pot going on your desk. Write in bed.

5. Put the project (chapter, section, page) aside for awhile. Work on a different writing (or nonwriting) project instead. If you prefer, work on the two projects simultaneously, or alternate between them.

6. Write something else that comes easily: a letter, a memo, a recipe. Then return to your original project.

7. Retype your last page, then keep going.

8. Meditate or exercise for half an hour or more, then return to your piece.

9. Distract yourself for awhile. Take a walk, see a movie, visit a friend. Get your conscious mind off the problem; your subconscious will keep working at it.

10. Brainstorm with other people, particularly other writers, either one at a time or in a group. Invite and consider fresh perspectives and ideas.

11. Sit quietly at your desk. Focus on the spot where you're stuck for a minute or two, then let go of that image or idea and let your mind wander wherever it wants to go. Often these wanderings will lead to something helpful.

12. Offer yourself a reward of something you like a great deal once you finish your project. When you're done, promptly collect that reward.

13. Try starting that section, or even the whole piece, over again — but use a different point of view, time, setting, dilemma, narrator, viewpoint, or central image or metaphor.

14. Keep writing, even if you're going nowhere. Let the piece wander or lose its way for awhile. If necessary, write nonsense for a bit — but keep going. Continue to push ahead until something clicks.

15. If you work well under pressure, set a *reasonable* deadline for solving your problem. Stick to it.

16. Stop writing altogether for a little while. Maybe you need a break to help you build up your creative momentum.

12 Tips on Titles

1. Your title should intrigue or attract potential readers, without misleading them or giving away too much about your piece.

2. A title should do more than merely restate your theme or intention. It should add meaning, depth, resonance, or a twist of its own.
3. A good title prepares the reader, either overtly or subliminally, for the piece that follows.
4. Titles do not have to be snappy or exciting. An understated title — such as Shirley Jackson's "The Lottery" — often works very well.
5. Ideally, your reader should see an additional significance or effect in your title once they have finished reading the piece — as, for example, in Sylvia Plath's *The Bell Jar*.
6. Most good titles indicate the tone of the piece that follows, usually by setting it in a few words. However, a title can also adopt the opposite tone for a deliberately humorous or ironic effect.
7. Often a quote, image, or idea from within your piece will make (or lead to) an excellent title.
8. Many writers find that the best way to title a piece is to finish it first, then read it over carefully to see what words, concepts, or images stick with them.
9. No matter how good your title is, there is a 50 percent chance that whoever publishes the piece will want to change it.
10. If a publisher does want to change your title, don't automatically say yes or no. Consider the publisher's ideas on their own merits. Discuss the title, ask for alternatives, suggest alternatives of your own, compromise, dicker, or hold your ground as necessary.
11. Use a subtitle whenever more explanation is necessary (it rarely is in fiction and poetry), or when a title simply won't do enough on its own. Don't hesitate to use a subtitle when one is called for, but don't use one gratuitously.
12. Contrary to widespread belief, essays intended for publication in scholarly or technical journals do not have to have colons in their titles.

3
Writing
Successful
Fiction

✔

✔

✔

The 8 Types of Fiction

1. **Novel.** An extended piece of fiction, normally at least 40,000 words long. Most novels have multiple characters, a central plot building up to an important climax near the end, and two or more subplots.
2. **Novella.** A mid-length work of fiction, shorter than a novel but longer than a short story — typically between 20,000 and 35,000 words. A novella normally has some complexity in plot and characterization, but has fewer characters than a novel and may lack subplots. Also known as the **short novel**.
3. **Short Story.** A short work of fiction, usually under 20,000 words. It is traditionally based on a single plot, event, character, or set of characters, and typically leads quickly to a climax and resolution.
4. **Short-Short Story.** A very brief story, usually 1,500 words or less. Most short-shorts are based entirely on a simple plot and end in a surprise, irony, or joke.
5. **Vignette.** A brief piece of fiction that vividly depicts or describes a person, place, or event. Vignettes need not (and typically do not) have a climax or much plot. Also called **slice of life**.
6. **Prose Poem.** A very brief piece of fiction, usually under 500 words, that emphasizes imagery, rhythm, and other elements of poetry.
7. **Anti-Story.** A work of fiction that takes the form of an essay or other nonfiction work. Examples: Jorge Luis Borge's "Funes, the Memorious" and Woody Allen's "The Irish Genius."
8. **Novelette.** Not a literary form at all, but simply a designation used by some magazines for short stories longer than 7,500 or 10,000 words.

Creating Three-Dimensional Characters

1. Think of each of your characters as a real person with a will of their own, not as a puppet for you to manipulate.
2. When a character's will conflicts with your own, let them have their own way — or replace them with a character

whose will naturally coincides with yours.

3. Give your characters the same kinds of choices that flesh-and-blood people have. Allow them to make their own decisions; then make sure they have to live with the consequences of those decisions, just as you and I do.

4. Deliberately avoid stereotypes, which can only weaken your piece.

5. Also avoid inverted stereotypes—standard stereotypes turned precisely upside down: the gruff, macho hairdresser; the generous-to-a-fault Scotsman; the intellectual, pipe-smoking garbageman, etc. These are just as one-dimensional as regular stereotypes.

6. Be wary when you find a character slipping "automatically" into a standard category—Japanese immigrants, window washers, New York Jews, Yale alumni, etc. Remove them from the standard groove and give them their own identity.

7. Focus on what makes each of your characters unique or unusual. Try to give each character at least two details that set them apart from other people (such as their love of old Mickey Rooney movies, their Fighting Quakers t-shirt, or their way of nodding when they're confused).

8. Try to show at least two sides of each character's personality. Often this can be done with two or three of the right details, gestures, or lines of dialogue.

9. Create characters who intrigue or fascinate *you*. If you're not interested in them as people, your reader isn't likely to be.

10. Remember that you don't have to like a character to want to write about them. Feel free to write about characters who irritate, disturb, or infuriate you. (Feel equally free to write about characters you admire, adore, or envy.)

11. Borrow intriguing character traits from real people. Also consider combining several such traits from several different people into a single character. For example, you might give a character your mother's habit of scratching her elbow when she's nervous; your husband's obsession with clean windows; your boss's worry about always having enough change for the parking meter; and your own lack of interest in fashion.

12. Keep in mind that not every character needs to be 3-D. Truly minor characters who appear only for a moment—to sell a

hot dog, hold open a door, or wave goodbye to a spouse — can be mere stick figures. However, often even these people can be brought completely to life with one vivid, unusual, or wonderfully appropriate detail.

12 Ways to Get to Know Your Characters Better

To better understand any one of your characters, pretend that they are not your own creation, but an actual flesh-and-blood person. Then imagine one or more of the following:

1. What would this person's resume or job application look like? What sort of a job would they be applying for? What kind of job might they have right now?
2. Where do they live? What does their home look like? Imagine the decor and furnishings in each room.
3. What are their favorite foods? What's inside the refrigerator and kitchen cabinets? What restaurants are they likely to go to, and what would they order?
4. What are their most treasured possessions, and why? How did they come to own each item?
5. What are their tastes in clothing, movies, TV, music, people, or anything else?
6. What makes this person unusual or unique? What sets them apart from everyone else?
7. Imagine the character is sitting across from you. What do they look like? How are they dressed? How are they sitting?
8. Start up an imaginary conversation with this person. Let them talk to you about whatever is on their mind. If you like, actually speak their words aloud. Listen to (and, if you wish, write down) what they say. Note their intonations, gestures, and facial expressions. Go ahead and insult them, compliment them, or start an argument, and see what they do.
9. Draw a realistic picture of the person. Then, if you like, draw a caricature as well.
10. Imagine your character in a variety of settings of your choice: a cocktail party, a formal dinner, an inner-city laundromat, a Pentecostal revival, a college dormitory, etc.

Turn them loose and watch what they do.

11. How would this person be described by their friends? Their family? Their employer? Their coworkers? A stranger watching them walk past?
12. Describe your characters as they see themselves. Then describe them as they really are.

Naming Your Characters

1. Consider the names of your characters carefully. The right names can add resonance, meaning, implication, and/or irony to a piece of writing.
2. Except in allegory, avoid names that telegraph overt messages to your readers or that are too obviously appropriate; they are more annoying than enlightening. Don't name a petty crook Carlton Swindle or a fellow with a shaved head Nathan Pate. Avoid overtly ironic names, too—e.g., a weightlifter named Lynn Tweedie.
3. Pick names that reflect the time, place, and culture (or subculture) you're writing about. If you're not sure what names are appropriate for a certain culture, do the necessary research to find out.
4. Remember that North Americans have an enormous range of names. People in Detroit, for example, are named things such as McCarthy, Minsky, Johansen, Klug, Beylerian, Ortega, Hakim, Singh, Wiggin, and Mead.
5. Watch out for names that could distract (or, worse, unintentionally amuse) your reader—e.g., McGilligan, Twitt, Popcorn, Kickernick. Find something that doesn't call so much attention to itself—unless calling attention to the name is precisely what you want to do.
6. Make your characters' names easy to tell apart. Readers (not to mention editors and typesetters) might confuse two characters named Betty and Patty—but they'd have no trouble with Betty and Patricia or Betty and Pat.
7. Steer clear of stereotyped names (unless you are dealing with a very closed and tightly-knit subculture that normally uses such names). Susan Fishman is more three-dimensional than Sarah Goldfarb; Jorge Cisneros is more interesting than Pedro Gonzalez.

8. Above all, your characters' names should feel right—just as your characters should feel like real people.

7 Ways to Tell a Story

A piece of fiction can be told through any one of these methods:

1. Third-person narration, as is used in fables, allegories, tall tales, and most novels. This has historically been, and still is, the most popular approach to storytelling.
2. First-person narration, in which the author or a fictional character appears as "I." Also very common.
3. Second-person narration, in which the reader becomes the protagonist. ("You enter the room and suddenly freeze.") Extremely rare, and usually difficult to pull off, but very engaging when done well.
4. Personal written records—diaries, journal entries, etc., written by one or more of your characters; or, letters written between two or more of them.
5. Impersonal written records—newspaper accounts, transcripts of speeches, teleprompter scripts, etc., from which the reader pieces together the tale.
6. Stream of consciousness. The reader follows a character's thoughts as they occur to him or her, as in portions of William Faulkner's *The Sound and the Fury*. When stream of consciousness takes the form of standard written English, as in Saul Bellow's *Mr. Sammler's Planet* or Virginia Woolf's *To the Lighthouse*, rather than a quasi-English flow of thoughts, it may be indistinguishable from third- or first-person narration.
7. Some combination of two or more of the above.

The 8 Types of Narrators

In fiction, the person or persona who tells the story is called the **narrator**. *In choosing the narrator or narrators for a work of fiction, you have eight options:*

1. **The Protagonist.** The story is told by the character within the piece around whom the story evolves and revolves. Example: Edgar Allan Poe's "The Cask of Amontillado."
2. **The Internal Observer.** The story is told by a character within the piece who observes the protagonist in action. Example: J.D. Salinger's "The Laughing Man."
3. **The External Observer.** The story is told by a character who has a distinct voice and personality, but who is not personally involved in the story they tell. Example: Mark Twain's "The Notorious Jumping Frog of Calaveras County."
4. **The Author.** The writer of the story takes the overt role of narrator, without disguise or artifice. Common in nonfiction; very rare in fiction.
5. **The False Author.** The narrator purports to be the writer, but in fact is just as fictional as the characters who populate the tale. Example: Kurt Vonnegut's *Breakfast of Champions*.
6. **The Nonentity.** The narrator is more or less invisible, and devoid of personality and persona, much like the narrator of a newspaper story. Events are clearly described, but they are not narrated by a recognizable voice or personality. Example: Shirley Jackson's "The Lottery."
7. **Multiple Narrators.** Different parts of the story are told by different characters, who are usually (but not necessarily) part of the story they tell. Example: William Faulkner's *As I Lay Dying*. In rare cases, portions may also be narrated by the author, a false author, or a nonentity.
8. **The Written Record.** The narrator is the fictional, and usually unmentioned and unnamed, author of some ostensibly factual (but of course fictional) written account, such as a newspaper story or court transcript, from which the reader gleans the story. Often several such narrators (and several different written records) appear in the same work of fiction. Quite rare.

9 Tips on Plotting

1. There is no one right way to plot a work of fiction. Indeed, often a writer uses several different methods to assemble a plot that feels right. Do what seems best for each piece.

2. Remember that your plot must fit your characters and settings. You might need to change either or both of these to make your plot work. Or you might choose to alter your plot and/or setting. (In practice, it's usually easier to redo a plot than to try to force everything else in your piece to fit it.)

3. Many writers outline their plots before they begin writing; others simply let their characters loose and watch what they do. Still others outline (either what they've already done, what they plan to do next, or both) only *after* they've finished a draft. All of these methods have worked for many writers.

4. An unusual but often highly effective option is to outline not what happens in your piece, but what effects you hope to have on your reader in each part of your tale.

5. If outlining doesn't appeal to you, try netlining: drawing a visual diagram of the images, characters, and events you want to use, and connecting items that relate with lines and arrows.

6. Keep your influence hidden as much as possible. Readers shouldn't be able to see you standing in the background, pulling your characters' strings. Everything that occurs should feel natural and appropriate—even the twists, ironies, and surprises.

7. You don't have to wrap up everything neatly in a work of fiction. In fact, if everything works out too perfectly (or too abysmally), it may seem forced or unbelievable. Real life is full of loose ends and less-than-ideal resolutions; keep a few of these in your fiction.

8. Look for events, developments, and twists that work in two or more ways at once, or that have multiple implications, meanings, or consequences. These can be among the most powerful elements in any piece of fiction.

9. Follow your hunches and intuitions, no matter how strange they might seem at first. They're usually right. (And if one of them isn't, you can simply change your direction.)

How to Show Instead of Tell

1. Keep in mind that good fiction reveals rather than explains. Your goal in each piece of fiction is to provide your reader with actual *experience*, not merely with concepts and outlines of events.
2. As you write a scene, imagine that you are there watching it unfold before you, step by step. Then write down what you experience—what you see, hear, touch, smell, and/or taste.
3. Reveal your characters primarily through their actions, not by telling your reader about them.
4. Remember that very little in this world is static and silent, including objects—even "stationary" objects. In a house, for example, the floors might creak, a screen door might fly open in the wind, and smoke might rise from the chimney. When you present an object or setting to readers, you can make it far more vivid by showing it in motion, along with any sounds and/or smells that result from that motion.
5. Get out of the way. Intrude with background, asides, and observations of your own as infrequently as possible.
6. Read each of your drafts carefully, aloud. If you can't experience a scene as if you were living through it yourself, work on it some more.

11 Keys to Handling Description

1. We experience the world through our five senses. Therefore, to create people, places, and events in your fiction that seem real, use words and phrases that create sensory impressions (also called **images**). In fiction, imagery + events = experience.
2. Give your readers the same sensory information and details that they would notice and find important if they were actually there, in the presence of what you're describing.
3. In general, use adjectives that describe (thick, salty, jangling, furry, speckled, sweet) rather than those that judge or evaluate (ugly, spectacular, annoying, breathtaking, pathetic), except when your own evaluation is absolutely necessary to your reader.

4. Combining imagery from two or more different senses can really bring a setting or scene to life. For example, if you need to describe a crowded amusement park, include not only the sights and sounds, but the smells (of cotton candy, popcorn, well-oiled machinery, hot asphalt, etc.).

5. More is not necessarily better. Usually it takes just a few details to bring a character, event, or place completely to life — but they must be just the right details. Consider carefully what sensory impressions are most significant or unique to whatever or whomever you're describing.

6. The sense of smell is the most powerful and evocative — and most neglected — of all our senses. Using it appropriately in your fiction can yield powerful results. (Recall, for example, how your mother's house — or your mother — usually smells.)

7. Choose details especially carefully when describing characters. Unless a character's height, build, hair color, or facial features are significant, don't describe them. Instead, focus on the kinds of details that are more revealing of your character's personality: the kind of shoes she likes to wear, what she does just before going to bed every night, or the way she raises her eyebrows when she's flattered or amused.

8. You don't have to make up every detail from scratch. Some of your best descriptions, images, and details will come from mining your memory. If you need to describe a fictional beauty salon, think about the real beauty salons you've visited. You may describe one of these actual salons, or combine elements from two or more different ones.

9. Consider combining the real and the unreal to create a vivid description or image. For example, when describing a hospital room, combine the humming overhead lights from one of your high school classrooms, the machinery from the intensive care unit where you work, and decor from your imagination.

10. As a general rule, choose the concrete and specific over the abstract or general.

11. There is no across-the-board "correct" amount of detail to use in a work of fiction. However, the following generality applies: use every bit of detail that your reader needs — and not a shred more.

Viewpoints in Fiction

There are five basic points of view to choose from when creating a work of fiction:

1. **The Omniscient Viewpoint.** The reader can observe any character or event the author chooses, and can know, at the author's whim, anything the author wants him or her to know. This might include a character's most private thoughts, their unconscious motivations, things they do not and cannot know, things that will take place in the future, and so on. Of necessity, pieces written with an omniscient point of view use the third person.

2. **The Repertorial Viewpoint.** Similar to the above, but with limitations on what the reader can know. Instead of being given omniscient powers, the reader is told only what the characters do and say; their thoughts and feelings remain private, although they may be implied by their actions. However, as with an omniscient viewpoint, the reader can travel throughout time and space at the author's discretion. Thus, the reader might watch as the Great Barrier Reef is formed, then follow the actions of several characters in the 1960s, then observe a circus that none of the characters in the tale has yet visited. Pieces with this viewpoint also employ the third person.

3. **The Internal Character Viewpoint.** The reader follows a single character throughout the piece, and is privy to what that character says, hears, sees, does, feels, and thinks. The piece may be written in the first or third person.

4. **The External Character Viewpoint.** The reader follows a single character throughout the piece, but cannot see inside his or her head. The reader's overt information is limited to what that character does and says—although their thoughts and feelings may be implied by their actions.

5. **Multiple Viewpoints.** At the author's discretion, the reader shifts from one character's point of view to another's.

10 Steps to Creating Effective Dialogue

1. Above all, *listen* — to other people's speech, to your own, and even to recorded messages. The people who write the best dialogue haven't mastered a special dialogue-writing technique; they've just learned how to listen.
2. Learn to eavesdrop on other people's conversations — tactfully and surreptitiously, of course. Speech is at its most natural when people aren't aware that they're being listened in on.
3. Pay special attention to inflections, accents, and diction that are related to a speaker's social, economic, and ethnic background. These are some of the most revealing aspects of dialogue.
4. Note buzzwords — words whose meanings are known only to members of a certain profession, ethnic group, club, family, or other group.
5. If you like, carry a tape recorder with you. Record people's speech and play it back, listening carefully.
6. As you write, don't try to build dialogue as if it were a birdhouse. Instead, replay in your head appropriate things you've heard in the past that have stuck with you. Listen to the voices you hear inside your head. Write down what they say, or at least use them for a guide.
7. Don't edit any dialogue as you write it. Let it flow naturally.
8. *After* you've finished a full draft of your piece (or scene, section, canto, etc.), read what you've written aloud, and listen to what you hear. If it doesn't sound right, rewrite it; then read and listen again. Repeat this process until you've got the words right.
9. A little bit of an accent or dialect goes a long way. "We was just sittin' here" has the right ring and is easy to read; "We wuz just a-sittin' hyar" overdoes things and becomes distracting. In particular, use apostrophes and odd spellings sparingly, only when necessary.
10. Authenticity is important, but it isn't everything. You want your dialogue to sound and feel real, but sometimes, for the sake of clarity and "realism," you'll need to tone some things down or make them closer to standard American English. This may mean sacrificing a bit of true authenticity

for something that *sounds* more authentic (but actually isn't).

Beginning and Ending Your Story

Writing Effective Beginnings

1. You don't have to write your opening scene first. Feel free to write later scenes — even your climax — first. Then, once you've immersed yourself in your tale, go back and write your opening.
2. Your story begins just before the central problem begins to emerge — no earlier. Provide only what background the reader needs to understand the problem and its significance; then start building the tension.
3. Remember that you've only got a few paragraphs to hook your reader. Give them something intriguing — an event, a setting, an image, an insight, a character, or an unusual style of writing — almost immediately.
4. Also remember that you *don't* have to start with a shock or surprise. Don't throw a gratuitous dead body at your reader, especially when an unexpected guest or a lucid observation might work just as well, or better.
5. A good opening should fit naturally with the rest of the piece. It should give your reader a sense (either overt or subliminal) of what is to come in the way of tone, mood, and events. It should *not* mislead your readers, intentionally or unintentionally.
6. Avoid using tricks or gimmicks in your opening, unless your whole piece is based on one.
7. Avoid expository lumps (long stretches of narration that explain what has happened in the past). Show your characters in action; don't bore your reader with explanations.
8. Even more strenuously avoid explanatory dialogue, where characters explain (ostensibly to each other, but in fact to the reader) what's been going on. ("Remember when we had breakfast this morning, Ted, and the waitress named Betty slapped you?")
9. After you've written your next-to-final draft, look closely at your story to see if you really need all of your opening scene.

Often your second scene (or the second half of scene one) will turn out to be the perfect beginning. Nevertheless, it may have been necessary for you to write the earlier material to get yourself fully involved with your characters and their situation.

Writing Strong Endings

1. Your ending must leave your readers satisfied—even if it is unhappy, unexpected, or inconclusive. Above all, your readers must feel the piece was worth their time and attention.
2. A good ending *feels* like an ending and has a sense of closure. Often this is produced by a change in locale, pacing, or level of tension.
3. Your ending must be appropriate for your piece. Avoid endings that aren't warranted by the events that precede it, or that are incompatible with a character's personality, motivations, or actions. If the reader can see you in the background orchestrating the conclusion, it needs more work.
4. You don't have to have a clear, snappy, or hard-hitting ending, and you don't have to make a point, teach a lesson, or cite a moral—though you may if you want to.
5. Let your characters' actions and situations reveal the significance of your ending. Don't explain what your story means or what your characters have learned ("Sherry knew, at last, that she could depend on her uncle"). Also avoid having your characters explain to each other what they have learned ("Todd, I've finally realized that I can truly depend on Uncle Arnie").
6. Pay special attention to your final sentence, image, and/or line of dialogue, because your readers certainly will.

19 Guidelines for Preparing a Novel Proposal

1. Remember that a novel proposal (sometimes called a **portion and outline**) is, first and foremost, a tool for selling your novel to a publisher. Everything about your proposal should make you and your book look as publishable and professional as possible.

2. Your proposal should include, at minimum:
   a. a cover page
   b. one sample chapter
   c. a narrative plot synopsis (called an **outline**) of most or all of the book
   d. an author biography
3. A novel proposal *may* (but need not) also include supporting materials such as endorsements from well-known people, photocopies (or a sheet of excerpts) of reviews of your work, and/or samples of your published fiction.
4. Throughout your proposal, use proper manuscript form and proper book format, as described in "14 Tips on Manuscript Form" on pages 101-102 and "16 Guidelines for Preparing a Book Manuscript" on pages 104-106.
5. Prepare a cover page according to the guidelines on pages 106-108.
6. Include as many chapters as you need to give readers a strong sense of the book's tone, mood, plot, and one or more major characters. In general, the more sample chapters, the better—especially if you haven't published a novel before. Most proposals contain the first one to five chapters, but you may use later and/or nonsequential chapters if they better present the book.
7. The core of your proposal will be your outline. This should synopsize the plot of the entire book—unless you include the opening chapter(s) as samples, in which case it may begin where the opening chapters end.
8. If you like, you may begin your outline with a series of very brief (at most, one paragraph) descriptions of your major characters. This is called a cast of characters page, and is optional.
9. Write your outline in the present tense. In it, focus primarily or entirely on plot and on external events, not on your characters' motivations or realizations or emotions. Avoid explaining your intentions as a writer. Stick to what happens to your characters. Be as detailed as you need to; good novel outlines have run as few as six pages and as many as forty-five.
10. Most outlines are written in the third person. However, if your novel is written in the first person, use either first or third person—whichever is more effective—in your outline.

11. Write an author biography for yourself, following the instructions on pages 108-110.
12. Put the following items together in a short stack: your cover page (on top); your author biography; your sample chapter(s); and, last, your outline. If you prefer, and if your outline synopsizes the entire novel, you may place the outline just before the sample chapter(s). Clip this material together with a large butterfly clamp.
13. Assemble your proposal in a neutral-colored two-pocket folder, the type without fasteners on the inside. In the left-hand pocket, place any endorsements, reviews, and/or samples of your published fiction, with the work samples last. In the right-hand pocket, place the cover page, author biography, sample chapter(s), and outline, in that order.
14. Type the title of your novel and your byline on a plain white label; affix this on the front cover of the folder, in the exact center.
15. Type your name, address, and phone number(s) on a second white label; affix this three inches below your title/byline label.
16. Attach your cover letter, unfolded and facing up, to the front cover with two small paper clips.
17. If your proposal is too lengthy to fit in a two-pocket folder, place everything in a typing-paper or manuscript box, in this order:
    a. cover letter
    b. endorsements, if any
    c. reviews, if any
    d. sample(s) of your published fiction, if any
    e. cover page
    f. author biography
    g. sample chapter(s)
    h. outline
    If your outline synopsizes the entire novel from beginning to end, you may reverse the order of these last two items. Type and affix labels on the front or lid of the box, according to the directions in items 14 and 15 above.
18. Keep in mind that not all novels lend themselves well to proposals (imagine a proposal for *Moby Dick* or *To the Lighthouse*). If your novel has little emphasis on plot, is difficult to synopsize, or simply doesn't look its best as a

proposal, finish the book before looking for a publisher for it.

19. See my book *Manuscript Submission* (Writer's Digest Books, 1990) for more detailed information on novel proposals, and for examples of novel outlines.

10 Tips on Writing Children's Fiction

1. Writing for children is fundamentally the same as writing for adults. The same general rules, approaches, methods, and options apply.
2. *Never* write down to children or underestimate their intelligence. Kids hate this — even if their parents don't mind.
3. Avoid cutesiness (e.g., "Oh, look, Andy Aardvark! There's Hortense Hyena in her lovely fur coat!") at all costs. Nothing turns kids off more. In fact, they tend to prefer funkiness (e.g., Teenage Mutant Ninja Turtles) and outright ugliness (e.g., Garbage Pail Kids).
4. Kids can usually handle fairly complex concepts and plots. Simplify something only when a full-grown adult might have some trouble following it.
5. The vocabulary in your piece should be appropriate for your readers, just as it should in a piece written for adults. Consider the reading level of your audience and avoid words, usages, and references its members are unlikely to know.
6. Kids' attention spans are usually shorter than adults'. The younger the child, the shorter the attention span. If a chapter, scene, description, or stretch of narration (or your entire piece) is running long, consider shortening it or breaking it into smaller, easier-to-read sections.
7. Children *can* handle difficult or touchy subjects. Indeed, in many cases some of those subjects are already parts of their lives. You may discuss such things as death, drug abuse, sexuality, violence, divorce, and even physical or sexual abuse in your work. You must, however, use an approach and a vocabulary appropriate for your readers.
8. Explicit sex and violence are clearly inappropriate for children. (Teenagers can usually handle them, although no

publisher of books or magazines for teenagers is currently willing to publish sexually explicit material.) Avoid anything prurient or deliberately lurid, except, perhaps, as parody, a la Monty Python.

9. Kids are far more willing than adults to accept the absurd, the fantastic, and the contradictory. For example, few kids would have a problem with the following opening: "Annie was the worst flyer in her class. Most of the other eighth graders had already been to the moon, but Annie could still barely hover above her desk." Most adults *would* have a problem with this, however.

10. Above all, remember that children are human beings. They have the same feelings, and many of the same concerns, as adults. Don't treat them as members of a separate, innocent, ignorant species.

4
Writing Successful Nonfiction

✔

✔

✔

11 Basic Principles of Nonfiction Writing

1. Be as clear, concise, and straightforward as possible. Violate this principle only when your piece clearly demands it.
2. Let your reader know in the first few paragraphs (in books, in the first few pages) what your piece will generally do, be, or contain. Also indicate what the piece's tone and approach will be. All of this may be done either overtly or by implication.
3. Ask yourself who your readers — and/or your ideal readers — are. Be sure your piece is directed toward them. If you like, draw up a profile of these people, either on paper or in your head.
4. Use the pyramid style unless your piece clearly requires something else. Start with a very brief explanation of who, what, when, where, and why; then answer the same questions in more detail; then delve deeply into your topic(s) with as much detail as your reader needs to get a complete picture.
5. Make sure that all your facts and quotes are accurate; check anything that you're not 100 percent sure is correct. A small slip may cost you some of your credibility; a large one could result in a lawsuit.
6. Clearly present all opinions and speculation as such — not as facts or probabilities.
7. Use the past tense unless there is a compelling reason not to.
8. As a rule, use specific details. When appropriate, use specific examples.
9. Give your readers something interesting or intriguing in your first paragraph or two (in books, in your first page) to hook their attention and keep them reading; but don't confuse or mislead them in the process.
10. Avoid extensive explanation or background in your opening paragraphs except when absolutely necessary. Most readers are more comfortable with being filled in gradually.
11. Your ending should do more than merely restate or emphasize your central premise. It should add a new idea, twist, premise, quote, or perspective that enables your

reader to come away from your piece thinking — and entertained.

The 20 Types of Nonfiction

Virtually every work of nonfiction prose fits one or more of the following categories. Each category includes works of all lengths, including books.

1. **News.** Provides a description of one or more specific events, as accurately and impartially as possible.
2. **Feature.** Offers an introduction to or overview of a particular topic. Its primary function is to provide information and insight, although it may be opinionated, partisan, and/or analytical.
3. **Analysis.** Provides basic facts and background, then interprets and analyzes that information. Most analysis pieces lead to a specific viewpoint, conclusion, suggestion, or opinion.
4. **Opinion.** Primarily intended to set forth the author's opinion, explain and defend it, and try to convince readers of it (or at least of its legitimacy).
5. **How-To.** Offers readers directions and guidance for completing a specific task or reaching a particular goal.
6. **Investigation.** An extensive, in-depth inquiry into a subject or event, in an attempt to uncover concealed or forgotten information and paint a new, more accurate picture of the topic.
7. **The Inspirational Piece.** Uplifts, inspires, and/or motivates the reader. Its specific content is often less important than the response it is meant to engender in the reader.
8. **Speculation.** Begins with a basic premise, fact, or body of information, then discusses what could happen or might be as a result. Most philosophy is speculation, analysis, or both.
9. **Interview.** The text of a conversation between two or more people, normally directed by the interviewer. Interviews are often edited or rearranged for clarity. One common variation is the **roundtable** — the text of a less organized discussion, usually between three or more people.

10. **Evaluation.** An overview, discussion, and judgment, often (though not necessarily) of a work of art. The review is the most common type of evaluation.

11. **Study.** A scientific, technical, professional, or scholarly investigation into a subject. Usually reports the results of a specific experiment, inquiry, or discovery.

12. **First-Person Narrative.** Describes in detail what happened to the author on one or more occasions. Often employs some of the techniques common to fiction. A first-person narrative that covers much or most of an author's life is an **autobiography**.

13. **Third-Person Narrative.** Describes in detail what happened to one person or group of people, often employing some fictional techniques. A third-person narrative that covers much or most of someone's life is a **biography**.

14. **History.** An overview of one event or a series of events, typically combining several of the above subgenres (analysis, feature, news, investigation, etc.). Includes **family history**.

15. **Journal.** All or part of a writer's journal, notebook, or diary, presented either edited or unedited.

16. **Observations.** A compilation of thoughts, aphorisms, and pithy comments on one or more subjects. Ambrose Bierce and Andy Rooney often employed this form.

17. **Creative Nonfiction.** A catch-all term for any nonfiction piece that shares some of the goals of fiction and/or poetry. May take almost any form (or combination of forms) on this list.

18. **Summary.** A presentation of information in deliberately condensed or distilled form. An **abstract** is a type of summary.

19. **List.** A simple item-by-item run-down of pieces of information.

20. **Satire.** Pokes fun at—or makes fun of—a person, event, belief, idea, or institution, often through exaggeration. **Parody** is a form of satire in which the piece purports to be or represent whatever (or the work of whomever) it is poking fun at. Satire may take virtually any of the above nineteen forms.

8 Steps to More Effective Research

1. Never make assumptions—even likely or highly likely ones. Check out every fact you intend to present as a fact, or else qualify it ("It seems likely that," etc.).

2. Cross-check your most important or significant information. Even "reliable" and often-relied-upon sources are sometimes wrong.

3. If you encounter contradictory information in two different sources, you might need to go back to *their* sources to resolve the contradiction. Don't hesitate to do this when necessary—your credibility may depend on it.

4. When possible, go directly to the original source, or as close to it as possible. In the long run, this often saves you time and legwork, and it's most likely to yield accurate information.

5. Never be afraid to ask anyone, no matter *how* busy or famous, for information. The worst they will say is no, and many will be willing to help. Often the people on their staffs will be happy to get you what you need.

6. Use the phone whenever possible. Instead of schlepping to the library, call the reference librarian. If you need several pieces of information, call four different libraries and get some of what you need from each.

7. Let one source lead you to another. Check and note bibliographies. When you speak to someone, your last question should be, "Do you know of any other person or resource that might be helpful?" When checking or compiling a list, ask each person or organization you contact to suggest additions to the list.

8. If a significant amount of time has passed between your original research and the time your piece goes to press, check your most important (and most changeable) information just before your deadline for making final corrections. This is especially important with books, where the time between completion of a manuscript and publication can be a year or more.

Conducting Interviews

Before the Interview

1. Make yourself knowledgeable. Get some background on your interviewee, and on the topics you'll likely discuss. Often the interviewee, or their staff, can provide much of this information.
2. Select a location that will have as little noise and as few distractions as possible.
3. Make a list of potential questions to ask. Organize these so that it is easy to skim through them or jump from one to another. Ideally, prepare more questions than you will have time to ask.
4. Equip yourself with everything you need:
   a. several pens or pencils
   b. one or two pads, with plenty of blank pages
   c. a portable tape recorder, complete with microphone and batteries with plenty of juice
   d. several blank tapes
   e. spare batteries
   f. your list of questions
   g. any supplementary or background materials you wish to have available
   h. a briefcase or other item to conveniently carry everything
   i. if you will be taking photographs, all your photographic equipment (including lenses, spare film, flash, etc.)
5. Dress appropriately for the person you'll be interviewing and the setting you'll be in. If you'll be conducting the interview at your subject's home, it's fine to dress casually; but if you'll be in a corporate office, wear a business suit.
6. Just before you leave for the interview, double-check that you have every item listed above. Also check to make sure that your tape recorder, tapes, batteries, pens, camera, etc. all work properly.

At the Interview

1. Introduce yourself politely and give the interviewee your business card. Get down to business within a few minutes.
2. Get comfortable and ask your interviewee to do the same.

If necessary, have water and glasses set out, or rearrange the standard seating.

3. Check the acoustics. As necessary, close the door or window, turn off a fan or radio, or move to another room.
4. Set up the tape recorder and microphone. Align the mike so that you can both speak into it without changing your position.
5. Have a five-second mock conversation to check the recorder. Make adjustments as necessary.
6. See if your interviewee has any preliminary requests or questions.
7. Agree on the approximate length of time the interview will last.
8. Begin the interview.
9. Direct the interview at first. As it progresses, take your cues from your interviewee's responses; alter the order of your questions, or the questions themselves, as appropriate.
10. Ask for clarification, explanation, or details whenever your interviewee says something vague or confusing.
11. Inform your interviewee when you have only a few minutes left.
12. At the conclusion of the interview, thank the interviewee for their time and responses. If you plan to send them a transcript of the interview for their approval, let them know when to expect it.

8 Ways to Tell If Your Book Idea Is Salable

The following checklist applies to both books and book proposals. It is a reliable guide, but it cannot make guaranteed predictions.

1. First, ask yourself who your audience is and why it will want to read your book. You can't sell your book until you can answer both of these questions.
2. Look carefully through the appropriate sections of several large bookstores to see what, if anything, is already available in book form on the subject.
3. Check the appropriate shelves and the subject section of the

card catalog in at least one *major* library for competitive titles.

4. Look in the most recent subject volumes of *Books in Print* and *Paperbound Books in Print*, as well as in the most recent *Books in Print Supplement* and the subject section of the latest edition of *Forthcoming Books*, for potentially competitive works. These reference sources are available in most libraries. If appropriate, also check *Subject Guide to Children's Books in Print, El-Hi Textbooks and Serials in Print, Religious and Inspirational Books and Serials in Print, Scientific and Technical Books and Serials in Print, Medical and Health Care Books and Serials in Print, International Legal Books in Print*, and/or *Canadian Books in Print*. If there appear to be any competing titles, note them.

5. Read copies of all competitive books that remain in print.

6. Ask yourself what makes your own book significantly different or better than every other book currently available on the subject. These differences will become your book's primary selling points.

7. If the answer to the above question is "nothing," your book is not salable as is. You will need to find and emphasize at least one *major* difference between your book and its competition if you wish to sell it.

8. Finally, ask yourself if your book is different or better in ways that will matter to your intended audience. If the answer is yes, your book has a good chance of selling— providing, of course, that it is written and organized well. If the answer is no, you'll need to find a difference that does matter to your potential readers.

17 Guidelines for Preparing a Nonfiction Book Proposal

1. Remember that a proposal (sometimes called a portion and outline) is, first and foremost, a tool for selling your book to a publisher. Everything about your proposal should make you and your book look as publishable and professional as possible.

2. Your proposal should include, at minimum:
   a. a cover page
   b. a detailed outline of each chapter

    c. an author biography

    d. an overview of the project

    e. a table of contents (unless the book will be a single continuous narrative made up of untitled chapters, as in a novel)

3. Unless you have already published at least two nonfiction books, or are already a nationally known authority on your book's topic, your proposal should also include at least one complete sample chapter (at least two chapters if each is less than ten pages). Chapters need not be sequential, and they need not be early ones. Include as many chapters as you need to give readers a strong sense of the book's tone and approach.

4. If your book will have an introduction, foreword, or preface that will be significant, and not merely an interesting forethought or acknowledgment of others' help, include it as a part of your proposal.

5. Your proposal *may* (but need not) also include supporting materials such as endorsements from well-known people, photocopies (or a sheet of excerpts) of reviews of your work, and/or samples of your published nonfiction.

6. Throughout your proposal use proper manuscript form, as described in "16 Guidelines for Preparing a Book Manuscript" on pages 104-106.

7. Prepare a cover page according to the guidelines on pages 106-108.

8. Write an author biography for yourself, following the instructions on pages 108-110.

9. Your overview is the most important part of your proposal. It should be one to three pages long and may be single-, 1½-, or double-spaced. In it, state the following as clearly and succinctly as possible:

    a. what the book is about

    b. why the book is important, useful, or necessary (sometimes called a rationale)

    c. who the book is for, and who will buy it

    d. what makes the book different from, or better than, every other book on the subject in print

    e. the book's "marketing handle": a description of the book in twenty words or less that includes the who, what, and why as described above

    f. a list of all competing titles, if any

    g. a description of what you can (or plan to) do to help promote the book (acquire endorsements, do readings and book signings, arrange local TV and radio appearances, etc.). This item is not absolutely required, but is extremely helpful — and strongly suggested.

10. Your outline must present a clear, thorough overview of your book's content. The outline for each chapter may be as long as you like, but no less than 100-150 words. Use whatever format works best: narrative paragraphs, bulleted lists of key points, a formal outline, etc.

11. If your chapters will be very short, or if your chapter titles clearly indicate each chapter's contents, you may do one or more of the following:

    a. outline your chapters far more briefly

    b. merge your outline and table of contents into a single item

    c. omit chapter outlines entirely

12. Put the following items together in a short stack, in the following order:

    a. cover page

    b. author biography

    c. overview

    d. table of contents

    e. introduction, preface, or foreword, if any

    f. sample chapter(s)

    g. chapter-by-chapter outline

If you prefer, place the outline just before the sample chapter(s). Clip all this material together with a large butterfly clamp.

13. Assemble your proposal in a neutral-colored two-pocket folder, the type without fasteners on the inside. In the left-hand pocket, place any endorsements, reviews, and/or samples of your published nonfiction, with the work samples last. In the right-hand pocket, place all the items listed in step 12 above, in the order indicated.

14. Type the title of your book, your subtitle (if any), and your byline on a plain white label; affix this on the front cover of the folder, in the exact center.

15. Type your name, address, and phone number(s) on a second

white label; affix this three inches below your title/byline label.

16. Attach your cover letter, unfolded and facing up, to the front cover with two small paper clips.

17. If your proposal is too lengthy to fit in a two-pocket folder, place everything in a typing-paper or manuscript box, in this order:
    a. cover letter
    b. endorsements, if any
    c. reviews, if any
    d. sample(s) of your published nonfiction, if any
    e. cover page
    f. author biography
    g. overview
    h. table of contents
    i. introduction, preface, or foreword, if any
    j. sample chapter(s)
    k. outline
    You may, if you wish, reverse the order of these last two items. Type and affix labels on the front or lid of the box according to the directions in steps 14 and 15 above.

5
Publishing Opportunities

✔

✔

✔

Types of Magazines

Consumer Magazines

1. Major general-interest magazines (*Vanity Fair, The Atlantic, The New Yorker, Saturday Evening Post*, etc.).
2. Major special-interest magazines (*Omni, Rolling Stone, Parents, Seventeen*, etc.).
3. Mid-size special-interest magazines (*New Age, Essence, Writer's Digest, PC Computing, Guideposts*, etc.).
4. Small special-interest magazines and newsletters (*Ghost Town Quarterly, American Dane, The Opera Companion, Paint Horse Journal*, etc.).
5. Men's magazines (*Esquire, Gallery, Gentleman's Quarterly, Swank*, etc.).
6. Women's magazines (*Ms., Ladies' Home Journal, Lear's, Savvy*, etc.).
7. Local/regional magazines, including newspaper weekend supplements (*Washingtonian, Yankee, Buffalo Spree, Southern Exposure*, etc.).
8. Children's magazines (*Cricket, Cobblestone, Humpty Dumpty's, Kid City*, etc.).
9. Popular fiction magazines (*Ellery Queen's Mystery Magazine, Fantasy and Science Fiction*, etc.).

Professional Journals

1. Trade magazines (*Signcraft, Electrical Contractor, Police Times, Hotel and Motel Management*, etc.).
2. Scholarly magazines (*Studies in Medievalism, Rhetorica, Renaissance Quarterly, Mark Twain Journal*, etc.).
3. Technical, scientific, and medical journals (*Lancet, American Medical Association Journal*, etc.).

Literary Magazines

1. Major literary magazines (*Paris Review, Triquarterly, North American Review, Grand Street*, etc.).
2. Small literary magazines (*Cream City Review, Lake Street Review, Pig Iron, Hibiscus*, etc.).

Types of Book Publishing

Book publishing firms are called **houses.** *A single house may publish two, three, or several different types of books.*

Many book publishers consist of several "houses within houses": semi-independent publishing arms called **divisions** *or* **imprints.** *(Knopf is an imprint of Random House; Writer's Digest Books is a division of F&W Publications.)*

Here is a breakdown of the different areas of book publishing:

Trade Books
These are books sold to consumers primarily through retail outlets—bookstores, discount stores, newsstands, etc.
1. Adult books (not erotica, but any book for adult readers)
2. Young adult books (for readers ages 12-16)
3. Children's books (also called **juveniles** or **junior books**)

Non-Trade Books
These are books sold primarily outside of bookstores and other retail channels.
1. Reference books (sold primarily to libraries and other institutions)
2. Business books
3. Medical books
4. Professional and technical books (books related to specific occupations and endeavors)—e.g., real estate, architecture, plumbing, college teaching—and sold primarily to people working in those areas.
5. Scholarly books (books intended primarily for academics and researchers)
6. Textbooks

Non-Books
Some book publishers also publish one or more of the following products:
1. Calendars
2. Audio tapes
3. Video tapes
4. Computer software

Book Formats
1. Hardcover (also called clothbound)
2. Trade paper (large-size paperbacks, usually printed on high-quality paper; also called quality paperbacks)
3. Mass-market paper (small paperbacks sold largely through newsstands, drugstores, supermarkets, etc.; also called pocket-size or rack-size books)

The Markets—Organized by Medium
Print Media
1. Books
2. Magazines
3. Newsletters
4. Newspapers
5. Greeting cards

Electronic Media
1. Television
2. Video
3. Radio
4. Audio tape
5. On-line services
6. Computer software
7. Audiovisual (filmstrips, etc.)

Performance Media
1. Film
2. Stage
3. Music (songs and lyrics)
4. Stand-up comedy (gags for comedians)

The Markets—Organized by Accessibility

10 = very easy to break in; 1 = very difficult to break in

10 weekly and small daily newspapers (including suburban and neighborhood papers)

9 Small special-interest magazines and newsletters

8 Mid-size special-interest magazines and newsletters
Local and regional magazines and newsletters

7 Scholarly books and journals
Trade magazines
Popular fiction magazines

6 Children's books
Reference books
Business books
Professional/technical books
Children's magazines
Small literary magazines
Big-city newspapers
Stand-up comedy (gags for comedians)

5 Textbooks
Medical books
Small and mid-size women's magazines
Technical, scientific, and medical journals
Greeting cards
Local cable TV
On-line services
Small-scale stage productions (local, college, etc.)
Local and college radio

4 Young adult books
Adult nonfiction books
Adult mystery novels
Adult romance novels
Adult science fiction and fantasy novels
Adult male adventure novels
Adult western novels
Adult horror novels
Major special-interest magazines
Small and mid-size men's magazines
Audio tape, audiovisual, film and video for business and industry
Songs and song lyrics (small-scale productions or

performances)
Computer software

3 Adult novels (nongenre)
Anthologies
Major off-Broadway stage production

2 Short story collections
Poetry collections
Major general-interest magazines
Major men's magazines
Major women's magazines
Major literary magazines
Local TV (except cable)
National radio
Short film

1 Network television
Full-length film
Broadway stage
Songs and song lyrics (major productions or performances)

The Markets—Organized by Rates of Payment

The following ratings are based on the typical number of dollars paid per manuscript page. These rankings are, of course, generalities.

Scale:
10 = $300 and up
 9 = $200-300
 8 = $150-200
 7 = $90-150
 6 = $65-90
 5 = $40-65
 4 = $20-40
 3 = $15-20
 2 = $5-15
 1 = $5 or less
 0 = no payment, or payment in copies only

Market		Rating
Full-length film		9-10
Network television		9-10
Broadway stage		7-10
Major general-interest magazines		5-10
Major women's magazines		5-9
Major men's magazines		5-9
Audio tape, audiovisual, film and video for business and industry		5-8
Major special-interest magazines		4-8
Adult romance novels:	advances	4-7
	total earnings	4-9
Small and mid-size men's magazines		3-6
Small and mid-size women's magazines		3-6
National radio		3-6
Adult male adventure novels:	advances	3-5
	total earnings	3-8
Adult horror novels:	advances	2-6
	total earnings	2-8
Anthologies:	advances	2-6
	total earnings	2-7
Children's magazines		2-6
Big-city newspapers		2-6
Adult science fiction and fantasy novels:	advances	2-5
	total earnings	2-10
Adult mystery novels:	advances	2-5
	total earnings	2-10
Mid-size special-interest magazines and newsletters		2-5
Major literary magazines		2-5
Young adult books:	advances	2-4
	total earnings	2-8
Adult western novels:	advances	2-4
	total earnings	2-7
Popular fiction magazines		1-6
Local and regional magazines and newsletters		1-6

Market		Rating
On-line services		1-6
Children's books:	advances	1-4
	total earnings	1-10
Greeting cards:	advances	1-4
	total earnings	1-10
Stand-up comedy (gags for comedians)		1-4
Local TV (except cable)		1-3
Adult novels (nongenre):	advances	0-10
	total earnings	1-10
Adult nonfiction books:	advances	0-10
	total earnings	1-10
Songs and song lyrics (major productions or performances)		0-10
Major off-Broadway stage productions		0-8
Business books:	advances	0-6
	total earnings	1-10
Computer software:	advances	0-6
	total earnings	1-10
Reference books:	advances	0-6
	total earnings	1-9
Technical, scientific, and medical journals		0-5
Short film		0-5
Medical books:	advances	0-5
	total earnings	1-10
Textbooks:	advances	0-4
	total earnings	1-10
Professional and technical books:	advances	0-4
	total earnings	1-8
Trade magazines		0-4
Small-scale stage production		0-4
Local cable TV		0-4
Small literary magazines		0-3
Songs and song lyrics (small-scale productions or performances)		0-3

Market		Rating
Short story collections:	advances	0-2
	total earnings	1-4
Scholarly books:	advances	0-2
	total earnings	1-4
Poetry collections:	advances	0-2
	total earnings	0-3
Small special-interest magazines and newsletters		0-2
Local and college radio		0-2
Weekly and small daily newspapers (including suburban and neighborhood papers)		0-2

9 Markets and Opportunities to Avoid

1. Any publisher that wants to charge for the "privilege" of publishing your work, regardless of its reason, sales pitch, or ostensible enthusiasm for your writing.
2. Any publisher that runs a display ad in a writers' magazine, a newspaper, or the Yellow Pages that begins, "Writers — Manuscripts Wanted," "Publish Your Book," "Become a Published Author," etc. These are almost always vanity presses. (See "10 Blunt Truths about Vanity Publishing" on the next page.)
3. Poetry anthologies that require you to purchase a copy of any book in which your work is published. This is a form of vanity publishing.
4. Writing contests that require an entry fee. The cash awards are small and the contests typically carry little or no prestige — they are just a way for the contest sponsor to make money.
5. Any market that charges a fee to consider your work for publication. This is outright extortion.
6. Any editor or market that has failed to respond at all (even with a rejection) to two previous submissions.
7. Any literary agent who charges a fee to consider, evaluate, or submit your work. A good agent makes money on commissions, not fees.
8. Any agent who insists on receiving a percentage of any

money you make from your writing, even if they weren't involved in the deal.

9. Any agent who requires you to sign a release before they will read your work.

10 Blunt Truths About Vanity Publishing

1. Vanity presses make a profit by charging authors to publish their works, not by selling books.
2. The vast majority of vanity press books sell very few copies and lose money for their authors. Those few that succeed usually do so because of extensive self-promotion by their authors.
3. Most book dealers and libraries buy very few vanity press books.
4. Vanity presses typically do very little to promote their books—unless the author foots the bill.
5. With few exceptions, vanity presses will accept for publication any manuscript that is not libelous, obscene, or overtly illiterate.
6. Vanity publishing is usually more expensive, and financially much riskier, than publishing and promoting your work yourself.
7. Some "regular" publishers—those that normally publish work at their own expense—will occasionally offer to publish a book *if* the author (or someone else) will put up a large chunk of money. This is sometimes called **subsidy publishing**. If you receive such an offer, turn it down—and never suggest this type of arrangement yourself. See item 10, below.
8. Publishing a book with a vanity press will have a *negative* impact on your writing career: many editors will consider you a gullible amateur.
9. Vanity publishing is completely legal.
10. For most writers interested in an alternative to mainstream publishing, self-publishing is a far better option than vanity publishing. See "13 Tips on Self-Publishing," on the next page, for an overview of this topic.

13 Tips on Self-Publishing

1. In the last few years, because of the development of software such as Pagemaker, self-publishing has become considerably easier and cheaper — and thus a more viable option for many writers.

2. Self-publishing is not vain or an admission that your work is not good enough to be published by a mainstream publisher. However, self-publishing work that is unfinished or not ready for publication *is* vain — and unfair to both your readers and you.

3. Self-publishing is an excellent option for material that has a highly specialized audience. Commercial publishers are usually unwilling to go after such audiences; but self-publishers can specifically target them with their promotion, publicity, and marketing efforts.

4. Before you publish your book, assess the market. Make sure there is a need for your book; that there is nothing else available quite like it; and that you know precisely who is likely to want, need, use, or buy it.

5. If you wish to make money from your self-publishing efforts (or simply wish to reach your audience and distribute your book(s) adequately), you *must* spend the time and money to promote yourself and your work. Promoting a single book can be a half-time job, but writers who have published their own work successfully — such as Peter McWilliams and Matt Groening (creator of "The Simpsons") — have almost all put immense amounts of time into promotion. See "Tips on Self-Promotion" on pages 135-137 for more details.

6. Don't skimp on quality. For your work to compete in the marketplace, it should be presented in an attractive, well-designed package. Spend the money to make sure your book looks good, and the time to check every detail and catch every error. If necessary, hire professionals to handle your design, layout, editing, and/or artwork.

7. Printers differ enormously in what they can do and what they charge, so shop around.

8. Advertise and publicize your book in the appropriate spots. Send out news releases and free copies to the appropriate people and organizations, particularly reviewers. Send out

galleys to prominent people to get their endorsements. Hire a publicist or assistant if necessary.

9. Getting your books into bookstores and other retail outlets takes a great deal of time and effort. Here are some options:
    a. Try to hook up with a distributor of small presses, such as Independent Publishers Group or Publishers Group West.
    b. Do a large flyer campaign to bookstores.
    c. Go store-to-store in your area; send flyers to booksellers elsewhere.
    d. Avoid bookstores entirely; focus instead on mail-order sales to individuals, libraries, and other organizations.

10. Make sure your book has an ISBN number, is properly copyrighted, and gets listed in *Forthcoming Books* and *Books in Print*.

11. Keep in mind that as a self-publisher, you will spend considerable time doing bookkeeping, ordering supplies, filling orders, and handling other details. Filling orders alone can eat up huge amounts of time. The more popular your book is, the more orders you will have to fill.

12. If your self-published book sells well, you can approach major publishers with it (either on your own or via an agent). Successful self-published books often go on to achieve publication with major presses.

13. For more details on self-publishing, consult one or more of the following books:
    a. *The Complete Guide to Self-Publishing* by Tom and Marilyn Ross (Writer's Digest Books)
    b. *How to Publish, Promote, and Sell Your Own Book* by Robert L. Holt (St. Martin's)
    c. *The Self-Publishing Manual* by Dan Poynter (Para Publishing)
    d. *1001 Ways to Market Your Books* by John Kremer (Ad-Lib Publications)
    e. *The Publish-It-Yourself Handbook* by Bill Henderson (Pushcart Press)
    f. *How to Get Happily Published* by Judith Appelbaum (HarperCollins)
    g. *Publishing, Promoting, and Selling Your Book for Self-Publishers and Impatient Writers* by John C. Bartone (ABBE Publishers' Association)

6
Finding Information and Support

✔

✔

✔

Researching Markets

*A **market** is any publication or organization that publishes, produces, or purchases freelance manuscripts. As a freelance writer with products (manuscripts) to sell, you need to research your potential markets carefully to determine which ones are most appropriate for each of your manuscripts. The better your market research, the better your chances for acceptance and success.*

1. Keep in mind the three most important rules for market research:
   a. It is an ongoing process — not something you can do once and be done with. You need to keep up with what markets are doing *now*.
   b. Each piece has its own unique content and audience, and thus requires its own market analysis.
   c. You are the best-qualified person in the world to thoroughly research the markets for your work.
2. Before you begin your market research for any piece, ask yourself these questions:
   a. Who is this piece written for?
   b. What does it do for them?
   c. What approach and/or format does it use to do this?
3. You can do excellent market research at the following locations:
   a. Libraries. Check reference works and industry magazines for information. Also look through the stacks, the periodical racks, the serials list, and the card catalog (or its computerized equivalent) for likely publishers and publications, similar or competitive titles, and other pertinent information. Large university libraries and main branches of big-city libraries are by far your best bets.
   b. Newsstands. Browse through the magazines and newspapers to find likely markets; browse through the books to locate likely publishers and similar or competing titles. Visit the largest newsstand you can.
   c. Bookstores. Follow the same procedures as at

newsstands. The larger the bookstore, the better.

    d. Your own home. Buy or borrow references to use at your convenience; use the phone to call libraries, bookstores, and other resources.

4. Remember that no two publishers or publications are exactly alike. It is not enough to decide that your piece is appropriate for, say, a women's magazine. *Ms., Playgirl, Good Housekeeping, Essence*, and *Vogue* are all women's magazines, but they run very different sorts of material. Even *Ellery Queen's Mystery Magazine* and *Alfred Hitchcock's Mystery Magazine* run significantly different kinds of stories.

5. Begin your market research by following the tips in item 3 above and using the appropriate resources in "35 Best Sources of Market Information," on pages 79-83. This will enable you to establish an initial pool of potential markets for each of your pieces.

6. Next, narrow your list to those markets that seem genuinely likely or possible. To accomplish this you must learn precisely what each market is publishing *now* — not last year or six months ago. Here are some guidelines:

    a. Magazines and newspapers: if at all possible, *read* one or two of the most recent issues. Check newsstands, libraries, inter-library loan, bookstores, etc.; if necessary, order a copy directly from the publisher.

    b. Books: get a copy of the publisher's *current* catalog. Check libraries and bookstores, or call the publisher and order your own copy (usually free). Or check the most recent "announcement" issues of *Publishers Weekly* and/or *Small Press* (page 82), and/or the most recent "new books" issues of *Library Journal* (page 81).

7. As you research a market, ask yourself the following questions:

    a. What audience or audiences does it seek to reach?

    b. What slant, focus, or bias does it have?

    c. What approach or approaches does it take?

    d. What themes or genres appear frequently?

    e. How long are the pieces it publishes?

8. Many magazines, book publishers, imprints, and lines (e.g., Harlequin's Intimate Moments series) publish **writers' guidelines**, also known as **spec sheets**. These explain

precisely what kinds of material that publisher, publication, or line is seeking. Writers' guidelines are available at no charge; just call or write the editorial department of the publication, publisher, or line in question (enclose a self-addressed, stamped envelope with written requests). Important: reading a spec sheet is no substitute for examining a current issue or catalog. When information on a spec sheet conflicts with your own research (as it will at times), believe your own research.

9. Update your research on any worthwhile market at least twice a year to familiarize yourself with any changes in its staff, audience, slant, focus, format, or address.

35 Best Sources of Market Information

1. *AWP Chronicle*. Newsletter published six times a year by the Associated Writing Programs, George Mason University, Tallwood House, Mail Stop 1E3, Fairfax, VA 22030, 703-993-4301. Provides market information on literary magazines and presses.

2. *The Bloomsbury Review*. Magazine published monthly at 1762 Emerson Street, Denver, CO 80218, 800-783-3338. Each issue contains many reviews of books of virtually every type; it's a good place to find out what sorts of books small and out-of-the-way publishers are doing.

3. *Books in Print* (Subject Guide). Reference book; published annually, with an annual supplement. Excellent reference source for learning which book publishers are doing which kinds of books. See also the subject guides to *Paperbound Books in Print, Children's Books in Print, El-Hi Textbooks and Serials in Print, Scientific and Technical Books and Serials in Print, Medical and Health Care Books and Serials in Print, The Small Press Record of Books in Print, Canadian Books in Print, International Books in Print*, and/ or *A to Zoo: Subject Access to Children's Picture Books*.

4. *Children's Writers & Illustrator's Market*. Reference book; published annually. A comprehensive guide to children's markets.

5. *Directory of Literary Magazines*. Reference book; published annually. Very useful for writers of poetry and

literary fiction.

6. *Directory of Poetry Publishers*. Reference book; published annually. Covers magazines and book publishers that do poetry.

7. *Directory of Publishing*. Reference book; published annually. A good list of book publishers in the United Kingdom and many other foreign countries, with fairly thorough information on each publisher.

8. *Dramatists Sourcebook*. Reference book; published annually. An excellent market resource for playwrights.

9. *Editor and Publisher International Yearbook*. Reference book; published annually. A list of many of the newspapers in North America and elsewhere, and the names of their editors.

10. *Forthcoming Books* (subject section). Bimonthly periodical in book form. Excellent reference source for learning which book publishers are doing books on certain topics. Available in virtually every library.

11. *Freelance Writer's Report*. Monthly newsletter, published by Cassell Communications, P.O. Box A, North Stratford, NH 03590, 800-351-9278. A good source of general market information.

12. *International Directory of Little Magazines and Small Presses*. Reference book; published annually. Covers both magazines and literary presses.

13. *International Literary Market Place*. Reference book; published annually. Includes a good list of book publishers (and their editors) outside of North America.

14. *Library Journal*. Magazine published twice monthly (monthly during certain months) by Cahners, 249 West 17th Street, New York, NY 10011, 800-677-6694. Provides information, through both text and ads, on what book publishers are publishing. Especially useful are the "announcements" issues, published for spring, summer, and fall.

15. *Literary Market Place*. Reference book; published annually. Contains an excellent list of American and Canadian publishers and their editors, as well as a list of book packagers.

16. *Member List*. Alliance of Resident Theatres/New York, 131

Varick Street, Room 904, New York, NY 10013, 212-989-5257. A list of some New York City markets for playwrights.

17. *Newsletters in Print*. Reference book; published every other year. Provides lots of useful information on many different newsletters.
18. *Novel and Short Story Writer's Market*. Reference book; published annually. A good guide to fiction markets.
19. *Oxbridge Directory of Newsletters*. Reference book; published annually. Another excellent resource for newsletter markets.
20. *Poet's Market*. Reference book; published annually. A very useful guide to magazines and book publishers that do poetry.
21. *Poets & Writers*. Magazine published every other month at 72 Spring Street, Suite 301, New York, NY 10012, 212-226-3586. Covers general markets.
22. *Publishers Directory*. Reference book; published annually. A good list of many book publishers, particularly noncommercial ones.
23. *Publishers Trade List Annual*. Reference book; published annually. A compendium of catalogs from many book publishers; useful for seeing what houses are publishing what types of books.
24. *Publishers Weekly*. Weekly magazine published by Cahners, 249 West 17th Street, New York, NY 10011, 800-456-9409. Provides extensive information, through both text and ads, on what many book publishers are doing. Especially useful are the spring, summer, and fall "announcements" issues.
25. *School Library Journal*. Published monthly by Cahners, 249 West 17th Street, New York, NY 10011. Provides an overview, through both text and ads, of what different presses are publishing for children and young adults, including textbooks and reference books as well as commercial fiction and nonfiction.
26. *Small Press*. Magazine published every other month at 121 East Front Street, Suite 401, Traverse City, MI 49684, 616-933-0445. Provides a good deal of information, through both text and ads, on what many small and medium-sized book publishers are doing. Especially useful are the spring

and fall "announcements" issues.

27. *Small Press Review*. Monthly magazine published by Dustbooks, P.O. Box 100, Paradise, CA 95967, 800-477-6110. Useful for learning what many literary presses are doing.
28. *Songwriter's Market*. Reference book; published annually. Very useful for songwriters.
29. *Theatre Directory*. Published annually. A good list of markets for playwrights.
30. *The Working Press of the Nation*. Reference book; published annually. Volume 1 is an excellent list of newspapers (and their editors) throughout the United States; Volume 2 is an equally good list of magazines and their editors.
31. *Writer's Digest*. Monthly magazine published by F&W Publications, 1507 Dana Avenue, Cincinnati, OH 45207, 800-333-0133. A good source of general market information.
32. *Writer's Market*. Reference book; published annually. A very useful guide to markets of all types.
33. *Writer's Yearbook*. Annual magazine published by F&W Publications, 1507 Dana Avenue, Cincinnati, OH 45207. No subscriptions; single issues only. Covers general markets.
34. Genre Newsletters. Newsletters that cover specific genres and areas of publishing (e.g., *Science Fiction Chronicle*) often contain excellent information on markets within those genres. So do newsletters published by professional organizations of genre writers (e.g., Mystery Writers of America).
35. Writers' Centers Newsletters. These often include useful market information; typically their focus is on literary magazines and presses.

Finding the Right Editors for Your Work

Once you know which markets to pursue, you need to locate the proper editor to approach at each market. If you send your manuscript to the wrong person, it may end up in the slush pile.

You want to get your piece into the hands of someone who has the power to accept your work and the willingness to read it— not a flunky who does an initial screening or a bigwig too busy working with literary superstars (or sales figures) to bother with your work.

1. To choose the right editor at a certain publisher or publication, you must find out who its editors are. Use the following resources:
   a. Magazines and newsletters: check the list of staff members, called the **masthead**, in the most recent issue. This is normally near the front.
   b. Book publishers: check *Literary Market Place*. If this fails, try one or more of the following: *Publishers Directory; International Directory of Little Magazines and Small Presses; Directory of Poetry Publishers; Writer's Market; Poet's Market; Novel and Short Story Writer's Market; Children's Writer's and Illustrator's Market*. News of personnel changes in book publishing appears regularly in the People column of *Publishers Weekly*.
   c. Newspapers: check the masthead on the editorial page; for weekend supplement editors, check the masthead within the supplement. If necessary, consult one or more of these books: *The Working Press of the Nation, Volume 1; Editor and Publisher International Yearbook*.
   d. Newsletters: consult *Newsletters In Print* and/or the *Oxbridge Directory of Newsletters*.
   e. Theatres: consult *Dramatists Sourcebook, Theatre Directory*, and/or the Alliance of Resident Theatres' *Member List*.
   f. Markets outside the United States and Canada: if you cannot get a copy of the publication or catalog, consult *International Literary Market Place* and/or *Directory of Publishing*.
2. If you prefer, or if the above resources don't provide you with the names you need, call the organization directly. If it's small, ask whomever answers, "Who's your ＿＿ editor?" or "Who's editing your ＿＿ line?" If it's a large

organization, first ask to be connected to the editorial department. Calling will often be necessary to locate department editors at large newspapers and editors of particular lines of books at multiline publishers. Also feel free to call to confirm that an editor is still with an organization. Whenever you get a name over the phone, confirm its spelling.

3. Once you have a list of potential editors, you need to pick one. Follow these rules of thumb:
    a. Whenever an appropriate department editor (automotive editor, poetry editor, food editor, etc.) is listed in a masthead or reference book, send your work to that editor. Exception: at very large magazines (but not newspapers) that have assistant or associate department editors, approach one of these people instead.
    b. When you must choose between people with titles such as managing editor, assistant editor, editor-in-chief, or acquisitions editor, consider the size of the publisher or publication. The smaller it is, the higher on the editorial totem pole you can go. If a magazine has only an editor-in-chief, a publisher, and an assistant editor, go with the editor-in-chief; if it also has a managing editor and a couple of associate editors, go with an associate editor.
    c. Never approach anyone lower than an assistant editor. And never send your work to a copy editor, production editor, or manuscript editor: selecting manuscripts is not part of these people's jobs.
    d. If you must choose between two or more people with the same job title at the same organization, play your hunch or flip a coin.
4. If you already know an editor, publisher, or producer at an appropriate market personally, of course feel free to send your piece to that person.
5. Keep in mind that some of the largest commercial book publishers and many TV and film producers simply do not consider unagented submissions. At these markets, your manuscript probably won't get read no matter who you send it to.

Useful Business Contacts

1. Editors
2. Literary agents
3. Other publishing people (such as publishers, art directors, marketing people, publicists, sales representatives, and photographers)
4. Secretaries and assistants of any of the people above
5. Bookstore owners and managers
6. College writing instructors
7. Librarians
8. Other writers (the more widely-published, the more useful they usually can be)
9. Arts administrators
10. Anyone famous, well known, or influential in any field
11. Anyone who is wealthy
12. Anyone who knows one or more people in any of the above categories. This group probably includes many people you already know.

What Business Contacts Can Do for You

Networking with others is not an absolute prerequisite for success as a writer, but it is usually quite important. Who you know does often make a difference—sometimes the difference between acceptance and rejection. Business contacts can:

1. Buy and publish your work.
2. Assign writing or editing projects to you.
3. Give you favorable treatment in considering your work (and/or your services as a writer).
4. Recommend your work or services to others.
5. Recommend other people and organizations to you, or even send them your way.
6. Give you advice, information, suggestions, and/or ideas.
7. Keep you informed about new markets and opportunities, and changes in current ones.
8. Tell you of their (and others') experiences with certain publishers, editors, or literary agents.

9. Help you find the right publisher(s) for your work.
10. Help you hook up with a good agent.
11. Tell you about job openings, and perhaps help you secure an interview.
12. Write endorsements and/or introductions for your work.
13. Keep you up on the scuttlebutt about certain publishers and people (regarding their financial positions, plans for the future, etc.).
14. Review your work fairly (and often favorably) in one or more media.
15. Hire you.
16. Write a reference for you.
17. Help you locate and/or arrange book signings, readings, speaking engagements, and other events.
18. Put you in touch with other people who can help you.

The 11 Best Places to Make Business Contacts

1. Writers' workshops and conferences
2. Special-interest conventions, such as those for particular literary genres (such as science fiction and mystery), academic conventions, and so on
3. The American Booksellers Association convention and the Canadian Booksellers Association convention, both held annually
4. Regional book fairs (such as The Great Midwestern Book Show)
5. Writing courses, particularly those that focus on publishing and/or professional writing
6. Readings and lectures
7. Writers' centers
8. Publication parties
9. Other literary events (bookstore openings, book signings, etc.)
10. People's offices (by prior appointment only)
11. Restaurants (by prior arrangement, at your invitation)

10 Guidelines for Asking Others for Help

1. Never be afraid to ask *anyone* for something small. But the more effort or time it takes to respond to your request, the more likely the answer is to be "no."
2. Be friendly, polite, tactful, and considerate of other people's needs at all times.
3. Don't grovel, whine, plead, demand, wheedle, or flatter. These approaches are sleazy and irritating, and they rarely work.
4. Be straightforward and up-front about what you need. Hedging or beating around the bush only wastes time.
5. If you want to speak with someone for more than a few minutes, offer to buy them a meal, a drink, or coffee or tea. Most people appreciate the gesture, and even the busiest people can usually fit a meal into their schedules, since they have to eat anyway.
6. Only ask for what you believe a person can reasonably provide.
7. Use the telephone whenever possible. Calls are far easier and faster to respond to than letters.
8. If you call and are asked to leave a message, include your name, phone number(s), *and reason for calling*. When possible, add that you will accept collect calls.
9. If your phone call is not returned within three days, call again. If you get no response after two calls, write a letter. (If your letter yields no response, write this person off.)
10. Always accept the answer "no" graciously.

Major Writers' Organizations of North America

United States

1. American Society of Journalists and Authors, 1501 Broadway, Suite 302, New York, NY 10036, 212-645-2368. For writers of nonfiction; there is a publication requirement for membership.
2. Associated Writing Programs, George Mason University, Tallwood House, Mail Stop 1E3, Fairfax, VA 22030, 703-993-4301. For college teachers of creative writing, students

in college writing programs, and others interested in writing and academia.

3. The Authors Guild, 330 West 42nd Street, 29th floor, New York, NY 10036, 212-563-5904. For writers of fiction, poetry, and nonfiction. There is a publication requirement for membership.

4. The Dramatists Guild, 234 West 44th Street, New York, NY 10036, 212-398-9366. For playwrights, composers, and lyricists.

5. International Women's Writing Guild, P.O. Box 810, Gracie Station, New York, NY 10028, 212-737-7536. For women writing in all genres.

6. National Writers Association, 1450 South Havana, Suite 424, Aurora, CO 80012, 303-751-7844. For all writers.

7. National Writers Union, 113 University Place, 6th Floor, New York, NY 10003, 212-254-0279, plus many local branches. For all writers.

8. New Dramatists, 424 West 44th Street, New York, NY 10036, 212-757-6960. For playwrights. Requires evidence of playwriting experience and ability, based on the submission of a full-length script, for membership.

9. PEN American Center, 568 Broadway, New York, NY 10012, 212-334-1660, plus branches worldwide. For people who have written or translated books of literary merit. There is a publication requirement for membership.

10. Poetry Society of America, 15 Gramercy Park South, New York, NY 10003, 212-254-9628. For poets.

11. Society of Children's Book Writers, 22736 Vanowen Street, Suite 106, West Hill, CA 91307, 818-888-8760. For writers and illustrators of material for children, both books and shorter works, and for anyone interested in children's literature.

12. Songwriters Guild of America, 1500 Harbor Boulevard, Weehawken, NJ 07087, 201-867-7603; 6430 Sunset Boulevard, Hollywood, CA 90028, 213-462-1108; 50 Music Square West, Suite 702, Nashville, TN 37203, 615-329-1782. For composers and lyricists. There is a publication or production requirement for full membership, but not for associate membership.

13. The Writer's Guild East, 555 West 57th Street, Suite 1230, New York, NY 10019, 212-757-4360 (for writers living east

of the Mississippi); The Writer's Guild West, 7000 West 3rd Street, Los Angeles, CA 90048, 213-951-4000 (for writers living west of the Mississippi). For writers of television, film, and radio. Members have normally sold at least one script.

Canada

1. Alliance of Canadian Cinema, Television and Radio Artists (ACCTRA)—Writers Guild, 2239 Yonge Street, 3rd floor, Toronto, ONT M4S 2B5, 416-489-1311, plus provincial branches. For writers of television, film, radio, and video. There is a production requirement for membership.
2. Canadian Authors Association, 27 Doxsee Avenue North, Campbellford, ONT K0L 1L0, 705-653-0323. For all writers.
3. Canadian Society of Children's Authors, Illustrators, and Performers (CANSCAIP), 35 Spadina Road, Toronto, ONT M5R 2S9, 416-515-1599. For writers of material for children. There is a publication requirement for full membership, but not for associate membership.
4. League of Canadian Poets, 54 Wolseley Street, 3rd floor, Toronto, ONT M5T 1A5, 416-504-1657. For poets. There is a publication requirement for membership.
5. PEN Canada Centre International, 24 Ryerson Avenue, Suite 309, Toronto, ONT M5T 2P3, 416-703-8448. For people who have written or translated books of literary merit in (or into) English. A second branch of PEN, located at 615 Rue Belmont, Bureau 212, Montreal, QUE H3B 2L8, 514-398-0946, serves writers who have written or translated books of literary merit in (or into) French. Both branches have a publication requirement for membership.
6. Periodical Writers Association of Canada, 54 Wolseley Street, 3rd floor, Toronto, ONT M5T 1A5, 416-504-1645. For writers of material for magazines, newsletters, and newspapers. There is a publication requirement for membership.
7. Playwrights Union of Canada, 54 Wolseley Street, 2nd floor, Toronto, ONT M5T 1A5, 416-703-0201. For playwrights. There is a production requirement for membership.
8. Writers Union of Canada, 3102 Main Street, 3rd floor, Vancouver, BC V5T 3G7, 604-874-1611. For writers of

books in all genres. There is a publication requirement for membership.

Writers' Centers

These organizations offer writers and the general public a wide range of services, including some or all of the following:

1. Information
2. Advocacy
3. Referrals (for job openings, professional services, etc.)
4. Conferences
5. Workshops
6. Seminars and classes
7. Readings
8. Open readings
9. Discussion groups
10. Library
11. Bookstore
12. Typesetting and/or printing facilities
13. Computer and/or word processor rental (on-premises)
14. Publication design
15. Lectures, panels, and/or talks
16. Storytelling
17. Lobbying on behalf of writers
18. Support groups
19. Manuscript criticism service
20. Grants and/or fellowships
21. Contests and/or awards
22. Publications (typically a regular newsletter, but in a few cases, books as well)
23. Discounts on books, magazines, typewriters, computers, and other products and services

National Centers
1. Poets & Writers, Inc., 72 Spring Street, Suite 301, New York, NY 10012, 212-226-3586. For all writers, especially writers of poetry and fiction.
2. Theatre Communications Group, 355 Lexington Avenue,

New York, NY 10017, 212-697-5230. For playwrights, composers, lyricists, and librettists.

Regional Centers

1. American Poetry Review, 1721 Walnut Street, Philadelphia, PA 19107, 215-496-0439.
2. Beyond Baroque Literary/Arts Center, 681 Venice Boulevard, P.O. Box 2727, Venice, CA 90291, 310-822-3006.
3. Greenfield Review Literary Center, 2 Middle Grove Road, P.O. Box 308, Greenfield Center, NY 12833, 518-584-1728.
4. Intersection for the Arts, 446 Valencia Street, San Francisco, CA 94103, 415-626-2787.
5. Just Buffalo, 2495 Main Street, Buffalo, NY 14214, 716-832-5400.
6. The Loft, 66 Malcolm Avenue S.E., Minneapolis, MN 55414, 612-379-8999.
7. The 92nd Street YM-YWHA Poetry Center, 1395 Lexington Avenue, New York, NY 10128, 212-415-5760.
8. North Carolina Writers' Network, P.O. Box 954, Carrboro, NC 27510, 919-967-9540.
9. Playwrights' Center, 2301 East Franklin Avenue, Minneapolis, MN 55406, 612-332-7481.
10. The Poetry Project at St. Mark's Church, 131 East 10th Street, New York, NY 10003, 212-674-0910.
11. Poetry Resource Center of Michigan, 111 East Kirby, Detroit, MI 48202, 313-972-5580.
12. Poets House, 72 Spring Street, 2nd floor, New York, NY 10012, 212-431-7920.
13. San Jose Poetry Center, %San Jose Museum of Art, 110 South Market Street, San Jose, CA 95113, 408-292-3254.
14. The Thurber House, 77 Jefferson Avenue, Columbus, OH 43215, 614-464-1082.
15. Walt Whitman International Poetry Center, 2nd and Cooper Streets, Camden, NJ 08102, 609-757-7276.
16. Woodland Pattern, 720 East Locust Street, Milwaukee, WI 53212, 414-263-5001.
17. Writers & Books, 740 University Avenue, Rochester, NY 14607, 716-473-2590.

18. The Writer's Center, 4508 Walsh Street, Bethesda, MD 20815, 301-654-8664.
19. Writers Connection, P.O. Box 24770, San Jose, CA 95154, 408-445-3600.
20. The Writers' Place, 122 State Street, Suite 607, Madison, WI 53703, 608-255-4030.
21. Writer's Voice, West Side YMCA, 5 West 63rd Street, New York, NY 10023, 212-787-4400.

Writers' Colonies

Writers' colonies offer writers a place to work without interruption or distraction. Residencies usually run three months or less (unless otherwise noted), and normally include a private room or cabin. Admission is usually competitive, and you must apply in advance (normally about six months ahead). Enclose a #10 SASE when requesting an application.

1. Edward Albee Foundation, 14 Harrison Street, New York, NY 10013, 212-226-2020. Housing (not meals) provided; no charge. The colony is in Montauk, Long Island.
2. Bellagio Center for the Arts, % Susan Garfield, The Rockefeller Foundation, 420 5th Avenue, New York, NY 10018, 212-852-8468. Meals and housing provided; no charge. The colony is on Lake Como in Italy.
3. Blue Mountain Center, Blue Mountain Lake, NY 12812, 518-352-7391. Meals and housing provided; no charge, though there is an application fee.
4. Centrum, P.O. Box 1158, Port Townsend, WA 98368, 360-385-3102. Housing (no meals) and a small stipend are provided; no charge.
5. Djerassi Foundation, 2325 Bear Gulch Road, Woodside, CA 94062, 415-851-8395. Meals and housing provided; no charge.
6. Dorland Mountain Arts Colony, P.O. Box 6, Temecula, CA 92593, 909-676-5039. Housing (no meals) provided; a weekly fee is charged; financial aid is available.
7. Dorset Colony House for Writers, P.O. Box 519, Dorset,

VT 05251, 802-867-5777. Housing (no meals) provided; a weekly contribution is requested.

8. Fine Arts Work Center, 24 Pearl Street, P.O. Box 565, Provincetown, MA 02657, 508-487-9960. Housing (no meals) and a monthly stipend are provided; no charge. Residencies run for seven months, from October 1 through May 1.

9. Hambridge Center, P.O. Box 339, Rabun Gap, GA 30568, 404-746-5718. Meals and housing provided; a weekly fee is charged; financial aid is available.

10. Leighton Studios, Banff Center, P.O. Box 1020, Station 22, Banff, Alberta T0L 0C0, Canada, 403-762-6180. Meals and housing provided; a fee is charged; financial aid is available.

11. MacDowell Colony, 100 High Street, Peterborough, NH 03458, 603-924-3886 or 212-535-9690. Meals and housing provided; a weekly fee is requested, but not required.

12. Millay Colony for the Arts, P.O. Box 3, Austerlitz, NY 12017, 518-392-3103. Meals and housing provided; no charge.

13. Niangua Colony, Route 1, Stoutland, MO 65567; no telephone. Meals and housing provided; a monthly fee is charged. Most residencies run two to eight weeks, but longer residencies are possible.

14. Northwood University Alden B. Dow Creativity Center, 3225 Cook Road, Midland, MI 48640, 517-837-4478. Meals, housing, and a small stipend provided; no charge.

15. Oregon Writers Colony House, P.O. Box 15200, Portland, OR 97215, 503-771-0428. Housing (no meals) provided; a weekly fee is charged; financial aid is available. Residencies are in a small lodge on the Oregon coast.

16. Palenville Interarts Colony, % Bond Street Theatre Coalition, 2 Bond Street, New York, NY 10012, 212-254-4614. Meals and housing provided; a weekly fee is charged; financial aid is available. The colony is in upstate New York.

17. Ragdale Foundation, 1260 North Green Bay Road, Lake Forest, IL 60045, 708-234-1063. Meals and housing provided; a weekly fee is charged; financial aid is available.

18. The Saint James Colony, P.O. Box 71, Saint James, MI 49782; no telephone. Meals and housing provided; no

charge, though a voluntary contribution is requested. The colony is on Beaver Island in Lake Michigan.

19. Ucross Foundation, 2836 U.S. Highway 14-16 East, Clearmont, WY 82835, 307-737-2291. Meals and housing provided; no charge.

20. Vermont Studio Center, P.O. Box 613NW, Johnson, VT 05656, 802-635-2727. Meals and housing provided; a monthly fee is charged; financial aid is available.

21. Villa Montalvo Artist Residency Program, P.O. Box 158, Saratoga, CA 95071, 408-741-3421. Housing (not meals) provided; a monthly fee is charged; financial aid is available.

22. Virginia Center for the Creative Arts, Box VCCA, Sweet Briar, VA 24595, 804-946-7236. Meals and housing provided; a daily fee is charged; financial aid is available.

23. Helene Wurlitzer Foundation, P.O. Box 545, Taos, NM 87571, 505-758-2413. Housing (no meals) provided; no charge. Residencies may extend to six months.

24. Yaddo, P.O. Box 395, Saratoga Springs, NY 12866, 518-584-0746. Meals and housing provided; no charge.

7

Doing Business
With Editors

✔

✔

✔

23 Common Misconceptions About Editors and Editing

1. Editors are your advocates and supporters.
2. Editors are your enemies.
3. You may not submit the same manuscript to more than one editor at a time.
4. You may not submit photocopied manuscripts.
5. All editors now accept (or expect) submissions on computer disks.
6. Proper manuscript form and other matters of etiquette and protocol aren't really that important, especially if you write well.
7. If your manuscript and cover letter aren't completely free of errors and absolutely correct in matters of grammar, punctuation, and form, your work will be summarily rejected.
8. Editors can, should, or will serve as guides, critics, teachers, or confidants to writers.
9. Editors critique (or are exptected to critique) most or all of the manuscripts they reject.
10. When an editor rejects a manuscript, they normally explain (or are expected to explain) why.
11. When an editor does critique a manuscript they've rejected, or explains why they've rejected it, their comments are usually sincere and carefully thought out.
12. Editors wield considerable power and make most of the decisions at the majority of publishing firms.
13. Editors usually set, rather than follow, publishing policy.
14. Editors, and not their superiors or their colleagues in marketing, decide which books get published and which ones don't.
15. Most editors actively seek, and are seriously interested in reading and publishing, unsolicited freelance material.
16. Most editors are more concerned with finding good writing than with filling predetermined slots or publishing material that fits their clearly-defined specs.
17. You must do whatever an editor says; if you don't, you may lose the sale and alienate that editor forever.
18. Asking an editor for more money or better terms can cost you the sale.

19. Many editors keep blacklists of people who have in some way disturbed or irritated them, and will never publish anything by any writer on such a list.
20. Most editors will work closely with writers to develop projects that require rethinking or rewriting.
21. Editors will rewrite promising but unpolished material.
22. Editors, especially book editors, won't buy any fiction unless it has sex and/or violence in it.
23. Editors will be impressed if you fax your manuscript or submit it via modem.

12 Common Misconceptions About Publishers and Publishing

1. If your work is good enough, it will eventually sell.
2. If you keep submitting a piece, it will eventually sell, even if it's not very good.
3. Most publishers look for and publish good writing, then do their best to market that writing, rather than first select an audience, then look for material to appeal to that audience.
4. Publishing is a gentleman's profession: genteel, sophisticated, and extremely considerate of writers.
5. The more publications someone has, or the more money they make from their writing, the better their work must be; the fewer their publications or the smaller their earnings, the worse their work must be.
6. No one buys (or reads) poetry (or short stories, memoirs, humor, first novels, literary fiction, etc.).
7. All bestsellers are rife with sex and violence.
8. Bestsellers have no literary merit and are inevitably forgotten within a few years.
9. Royalty statements are usually fraudulent.
10. Most royalty statements are both honest and accurate.
11. Most major book publishers are independent organizations, rather than parts of huge (and often international) conglomerates.
12. Most publishers are rolling in money.

The 22 Kinds of Editors

1. **Acquisitions (or Acquiring) Editor.** Primarily responsible for soliciting, evaluating, purchasing, and (usually) editing manuscripts.
2. **Assistant Editor, Associate Editor, Associate Department Editor, etc.** Ambiguous. Can be anything from a secretary to a copy editor to an acquisitions editor.
3. **Book Packager.** A person or organization that provides publishing services (such as design or production), finished manuscripts, and, in some cases, printed, bound books to large book publishers. The term **book producer** is synonymous.
4. **Consulting Editor.** Usually a freelance editor hired to offer advice and expertise. Occasionally oversees a project. In some cases the title is honorary, given to a well-known figure to add prestige to the publication.
5. **Contributing Editor.** 1) Someone who writes regularly for a publication and has some editing duties as well; 2) Someone who writes regularly for a publication but does no actual editing; the title is honorary and is awarded as a perk.
6. **Copy Editor.** Reads through manuscripts word by word, making changes and corrections. Sometimes called **manuscript editor.**
7. **Department Editor.** A person in charge of the editorial content of one department, genre, series, or section.
8. **Editor.** A generic term; can refer to anyone involved in the editorial function of publishing.
9. **Editor-at-large.** 1) A staff editor who handles a variety of tasks and wears several different hats, depending on the circumstances; 2) A freelance editor; 3) A consulting editor.
10. **Editor-in-Chief.** Someone in charge of the entire editing function at a publication—or of one entire line, area, imprint, or division at a book publishing house. The term **editorial director** is synonymous.
11. **Editorial Assistant** or **Editorial Associate.** Usually an editor's assistant; duties may range from those of a secretary to those of a full-fledged editor.
12. **Editorial Board Member.** Part of a board that, as a group, selects manuscripts for publication. This person may also

help determine editorial policy. Editorial boards are common among literary magazines and professional, technical, and scholarly journals; they are rare elsewhere. Occasionally the title is honorary (see **consulting editor**).

13. **Executive Editor.** Ambiguous. Synonymous with either senior editor, editor-in-chief, or managing editor, depending on the publisher or publication.

14. **Freelance Editor.** Hired by a publisher as an independent contractor to serve as an editor on a project-by-project basis.

15. **Managing Editor.** Oversees the day-to-day operations of a publication, publishing firm, or editorial department; often serves as the editor-in-chief's right-hand person.

16. **Production Editor.** In charge of the physical production of a publication, including printing, design, etc.

17. **Project Editor.** Supervises a particular publishing project.

18. **Proofreader.** Reads manuscripts and/or typeset material to check for errors in spelling, grammar, typesetting, etc. Does little or no editing.

19. **Publisher.** The person in charge of everything that goes on at a publication or publishing firm. Oversees the editorial department and all other functions.

20. **Reader.** Screens unsolicited manuscripts (those in the "slush pile"); rejects most and passes on the more promising ones to an editor. Sometimes called **manuscript reader** or **first reader**.

21. **Senior Editor.** Usually an acquisitions editor with a good deal of decision-making (and sometimes policy-making) power.

22. **Supervising Editor.** Ambiguous. Synonymous with either **managing editor** or (more often) **project editor**.

5 Ways to Keep Your Work Out of the Slush Pile

The "slush pile" is the group of manuscripts set aside to receive the last and least careful consideration.

1. Above all, write to editors *by name*, not merely by title. If you don't know an editor's name, find it out by checking a reference book or masthead, or by calling the publisher.

2. Choose the proper editors at the right markets; see "Finding the Right Editors for Your Work" on pages 83-85.
3. Follow proper manuscript form; see "14 Tips on Manuscript Form" below.
4. Prepare a well-written, carefully-typed cover letter according to the guidelines on pages 111-113. Be sure to inform the editor of your previous sales, publications, and other successes as a writer.
5. Put together a submission package that looks as professional and well-produced as possible.

14 Tips on Manuscript Form

1. Prepare your manuscript on a letter-quality typewriter, word processor, or printer, using a clear, dark, black ribbon or a laser jet.
2. Use a standard, easy-to-read typeface (*not* Script, Quadro, Gothic, etc.).
3. Use either pica or elite type (10- or 12-pitch)—nothing larger or smaller.
4. Use plain, white, unlined, medium-weight (16- or 20-pound), 8½" × 11" paper.
5. Type or print on one side of the page only.
6. Use margins of about one inch on all four sides. Leave the right margin unjustified.
7. Place a page heading in the upper left or right of each page (except for page 1 in a short manuscript or the cover page of a book or book proposal). This should include the page number and one of the following: a) your last name, b) the title of your piece, or c) a key word or group of words from your title. Begin your text three or four lines below the heading.
8. Do *not* include your social security number, the rights you are selling, or a copyright notice on your manuscript. These are unnecessary and amateurish additions.
9. Do not type "End," "The End," or "30" at the conclusion of your manuscript; simply end it.
10. Proofread and correct your manuscript carefully. Retype sections or pages as necessary.
11. Keep your manuscript clean, neat, and easy to read. You

may make some small corrections by hand. If a page requires a large correction, or more than two or three small ones, type or print out a new, corrected page. If you prefer, make corrections using correction tape, or scissors and transparent tape, and photocopy the new, corrected page.

12. If you have used a continuous paper feed when printing your manuscript, separate all the pages and remove the feeder strips from both sides.

13. Photocopy your manuscript; keep the original and submit copies.

14. Do not staple or bind manuscripts. Clip manuscripts of less than eighty pages with a paper clip or butterfly clamp; longer manuscripts should be placed in manuscript or typing paper boxes, available at office supply stores and copy and print shops. Exceptions are scripts for TV, film, radio, video, stage, or AV production, which should normally be bound; see *The Writer's Digest Guide to Manuscript Formats* by Dian Dincin Buchman and Seli Groves (Writer's Digest Books) for details on preparing scripts.

8 Guidelines for Preparing a Prose Manuscript

1. Double-space your entire manuscript, except for the upper third of your first page, which should be single-spaced.

2. In the upper left of page one, type or print out the following information, flush left, with each item or set of items on a new line:
   a. Your name (not your pseudonym)
   b. Street address, R.F.D. number, or P.O. box number
   c. City; state or province; zip or postal code; country (only if the manuscript will be sent to another country)
   d. Phone number(s); indicate which is work and which is home

3. If you have one or more coauthors, list all the collaborators' names, one per line, first. Choose one address as your mailing address and one person's phone number(s) as your "official" number(s); list these as in item 2 above.

4. If you are a member of a *pertinent* organization of

professional writers (e.g., Western Writers of America, Society of American Travel Writers, Authors Guild), indicate your membership two lines below your phone number(s), flush left, in this manner: Member, _____. If you wish to list a second membership, do so, flush left, on the line below. Do not indicate membership in any clubs, union, or nonprofessional associations.

5. In the upper right, flush right, indicate the approximate number of words in your manuscript, using this language: About _____ words. Round off to the nearest 100 words for manuscripts of 2,000 words or less; to the nearest 500 words for manuscripts of 2,000 to 10,000 words; and to the nearest 1,000 words for longer manuscripts.

6. In the exact center of your page, type your title, either in all capitals or both capital and small letters.

7. Two lines below your title, centered, type your byline, either real or pseudonymous, in this manner: by _____.

8. Begin your double-spaced text four lines below your byline.

6 Guidelines for Preparing a Poetry Manuscript

1. Type each poem, no matter how short, on a separate page.
2. Your poem may be either single-spaced (double-spaced between stanzas), or 1½-spaced (2½-spaced between stanzas).
3. In the upper left (flush left) *or* the upper right (flush left against an imaginary margin three inches from the right edge of the page), type the following information, single-spaced, one item or set of items per line:
   a. Your name (not your pseudonym)
   b. Street address, R.F.D. number, or P.O. box
   c. City; state or province; zip or postal code; country (if the manuscript will be sent to another country)
4. Drop down four lines; type the title of the poem, flush left, in all capitals.
5. Drop down three more lines and begin the text of the poem.
6. Do *not* list any byline, pseudonym, word or page count, or organizational or institutional affiliation. After the poem has been accepted for publication, you may instruct your editor to publish it under your pen name. (If you have already

established a reputation under your pseudonym, however, you may mention your pen name in your cover letter.) You *may* list your pen name as your byline on the cover page of a poetry *book*; see "Format for a Cover Page" on pages 106-108 for details.

16 Guidelines for Preparing a Book Manuscript

Follow the instructions below when preparing a book manuscript for submission. For guidelines on preparing a book proposal, see pages 48-51 (for a novel) or pages 60-63 (for a nonfiction book).

1. Your manuscript must contain, at minimum, the following items:
   a. a cover page
   b. an author biography
   c. the text of your book itself
2. It *may* (but need not) also include one or more of the following:
   a. illustrations
   b. an introduction, foreword, and/or preface (by you or someone else)
   c. a table of contents
   d. endorsements from well-known people
   e. photocopies (or a sheet of excerpts) of reviews of your work
3. Throughout your book, use proper manuscript form, as described in "14 Tips on Manuscript Form" on pages 101-102.
4. Double-space prose manuscripts; poetry manuscripts should be single-spaced (double-spaced between stanzas) or 1½-spaced (2½-spaced between stanzas).
5. Your table of contents, endorsements, or excerpts of reviews may be either 1½-spaced or double-spaced.
6. Prepare your cover page according to the guidelines on pages 106-108.
7. Prepare your author biography according to the guidelines on pages 108-110.

8. Assemble the components of your book in this order:
   a. cover page
   b. author biography
   c. endorsements from well-known people, if any
   d. reviews (or excerpts of reviews), if any
   e. table of contents, if any
   f. introduction, foreword, and/or preface
   g. the main text of your book
9. Begin each chapter, section, story, essay, or poem on a new page.
10. Number each page except your cover page. Page 1 will be the page following your cover page.
11. Number all pages of the book consecutively from beginning to end. Do not start counting again at the beginning of each new story, poem, essay, section, or chapter.
12. If your manuscript includes illustrations, follow these guidelines:
    a. Each illustration or photograph should be on a separate $8\frac{1}{2}'' \times 11''$ page, with a caption, photo credit, or illustration credit at the bottom (or, if necessary, on the back).
    b. Integrate illustrations with your text, in the approximate places where you wish them to appear.
    c. Number illustrations consecutively: illustration 1, illustration 2, etc.
    d. If an illustration follows page 23, number the illustration page 23a; if two pages of illustrations follow page 67, number those pages 67a and 67b.
    e. Illustrations smaller than $8\frac{1}{2}'' \times 11''$ should be attached to $8\frac{1}{2}'' \times 11''$ pages. If possible, enlarge any illustration smaller than $5'' \times 7''$.
    f. If you prefer, send slides instead of photographs or drawings. Place these in plastic sheets and include them at the end of your manuscript. Append a separate page of captions and/or illustration or photo credits. Number all slides, captions, and credits, and indicate where they belong in the manuscript.
    g. Keep the originals of any artwork; keep copies of all negatives to slides.
13. Place everything—unbound, unclipped, and unstapled—in a typing paper box or manuscript box. These are available

at many office supply stores, copy shops, and print shops.

14. Very short manuscripts — those of eighty pages or less — may be placed in two-pocket folders, as if they were book proposals. Follow the guidelines on pages 48-51 (for fiction) or 60-63 (for nonfiction).

15. On a plain white label, type the title of your book in all capitals; two lines below, type your subtitle, if any; two lines below your title or subtitle, type your byline. Affix this label to the top of your typing paper box or the front of your manuscript box, in the exact center. (If you are using a two-pocket folder, affix it in the exact center of the front cover.)

16. On a second white label, type your name (not your pseudonym), your address, and your phone number(s), each item or set of items on a separate line. Affix this label three inches directly below the title/byline label.

Format for a Cover Page

Follow these guidelines for preparing a cover page for a book or book proposal:

1. Use margins of about one inch on all sides.
2. In the upper left, flush left, type or print out the following information, with each item or items on a new line:
   a. Your name (not your pseudonym)
   b. Street address, R.F.D. number, or P.O. box number
   c. City; state or province; zip or postal code; country (only if the manuscript will be sent out of the country)
   d. Phone number(s); indicate which is work and which is home
3. If you have one or more coauthors, list all the collaborators' names, one per line, first. Choose one address as your official mailing address and one person's phone number(s); list these as in item 2 above.
4. If you are a member of a *pertinent* organization of professional writers (e.g., Western Writers of America, Society of American Travel Writers, Authors Guild), indicate your membership two lines below your phone number(s), flush left, in this manner: Member, _____. If

you wish to list a second membership, do so, flush left, on the line below. Do not indicate memberships in any clubs, union, or nonprofessional associations. Exception: if your book or proposal is a work of poetry, do not list any organizational affiliation.

5. If an agent will be submitting the manuscript, type or print out the following information in the upper right, one item or set of items per line:
    a. Your agent's name
    b. The name of the agency they work for (unless the agency bears their name)
    c. The agent's street address or P.O. box
    d. The agent's city; state or province; zip or postal code; country (if appropriate)
    e. The agent's phone number.
    This information should be typed flush left against an imaginary margin three inches from the right edge of the page.

6. If the manuscript is being submitted by an agent, you may, if you prefer, omit your own address and phone number(s). Instead, in the upper left of the page, on the line below your name, type "c/o" and your agent's name. Immediately below this line, type the information in 5b-5e above, single-spaced and flush left. Leave the upper right of the page blank.

7. In the exact center of your cover page, type your title in all capitals. If there is a subtitle, type this two lines further down, centered, in both uppercase and lowercase letters.

8. Type your byline two lines below your title or subtitle, centered, in this manner: by _____. If you wish to use a pseudonym, add it here.

9. If you have a prose manuscript, drop down ten lines and type the following information, centered: Approximate length: _____ words. In the case of a book proposal for a prose book, type "Projected" instead of "Approximate." Round off to the nearest 5,000 words (to the nearest 1,000 for books under 20,000 words). Do not indicate approximate or projected length for books of poetry or for very short prose works (such as children's picture books, adult books that are primarily illustrations, etc.).

10. A cover page is not required for any prose or poetic work

of less than book length. You may, however, use a cover page if you wish, for short prose works, for poem cycles, or for very long poems (those running six pages or more). Follow the guidelines above. However, for a poetry manuscript, do not include a line indicating word-length.

11. Scripts for TV, film, stage, radio, video, and AV material also require cover pages, but each genre employs a slightly different format. See *The Writer's Digest Guide to Manuscript Formats* by Dian Dincin Buchman and Seli Groves (Writer's Digest Books) for details on each of these.

Writing an Author Biography

1. Use an author biography in the following situations:
   a. To accompany the submission of a book or book proposal to an editor or agent.
   b. To provide an editor who has accepted a piece for publication with biographical information, which can be run along with your piece.
2. Your author biography should run between 50 and 400 words. The standard length is 200 to 250 words.
3. Double- or 1½-space your biography. In no case should it run more than one full page.
4. Write your entire biography in the third person. Use present tense except when another tense is clearly called for.
5. The primary purpose of your biography is to make yourself look as experienced, skilled, knowledgeable, or professional as possible. It should substantiate your claim to expertise on your subject and/or your strong ability as a writer.
6. Devote much or most of your biography to listing your writing achievements. Include some or all of the following:
   a. Your previous sales and publications. (If you have been widely published, list only your major or most relevant ones.)
   b. Specific (and favorable) facts about pieces you've previously published (for example, a poem has been reprinted in an anthology, or a book has gone into a fourth printing and sold 10,000 copies).
   c. Any *significant* writing awards or fellowships you've received.

d. Any other significant and relevant writing experience you may have (e.g., work as a public relations writer or political speechwriter).
  e. Any significant and clearly related advanced study in writing you've completed (such as a Master of Fine Arts degree in poetry from the University of Iowa).
  f. One or two very brief (ten words or shorter), highly favorable quotes taken from reviews of your previous work.
7. Also include any background information directly relevant to your piece. For example, if your piece is about jumbo jets, mention your years of experience as a jumbo jet mechanic. If you've written a health book, list all your medical credentials.
8. Do not mention your membership in any writers' organization here. You may, however, mention your membership in any professional organization that will help to establish your expertise in your subject.
9. Mention any significant publicity or promotion you have received, such as appearances on national TV or radio programs, or interviews with you that have appeared in national magazines.
10. Present all information as favorably as possible. For example, if you've published two pieces in small newspapers and two poems in literary magazines, you might write, "Her work has appeared in several magazines and newspapers throughout the United States, most recently in *The Gamut*."
11. Do not make an overt sales pitch. Stick to the facts; avoid complimenting yourself.
12. List only those credentials or publications likely to impress your editor, agent, or readers. For example, editors of literary magazines will be unimpressed—or negatively impressed—by your sale of a Harlequin romance.
13. Do not lie, distort the facts, or mislead your reader in any way.
14. The tone of your biography should suit your piece. If you've written a very cerebral book, write a terse, serious biography; if you've written a very silly piece, make your biography silly, too.
15. You will need to write a new author biography for each new

piece, or at least make appropriate modifications in your basic biography.

16. If you have few credentials and little experience worth mentioning, make your author biography brief—e.g., "Susan Swift is a short story writer living in Vancouver. She is currently at work on a long novel set in the Pacific Northwest." If (and only if) you have nothing to say about yourself at all, you may omit an author biography entirely.

17. See the second page of this book for an example of an author biography.

18. Include a condensed version of your biography (from 30-100 words) in any cover letter. See "Writing a Cover Letter" on pages 111-113 for more details.

19. When two or more authors (or a writer and an illustrator or photographer) have collaborated on a piece, there should be an author biography for each. Include both (or all) biographies on a single page; shorten them if necessary to make them fit.

20. If you've written a book that has an introduction by someone else, do a biography for each of you; the biography of the author of the introduction should go last. Both or all of these biographies should fit on a single page.

21. If you are using a pseudonym, you may do any of the following:

    a. Use your real name in your biography. Explain in the biography that you've used a pseudonym as your byline. (This information will be published with your piece unless you request otherwise.)

    b. Use your pseudonym in your biography; indicate that it is not your real name, but do not reveal what your real name is. You may still list all your credentials and experience, including pieces published under your own name (or another pen name), if you wish.

    c. Use your pseudonym in your biography, but do not indicate that it is not your real name. You may list all your credentials and experience, including (if you wish) pieces published under your own name or another pseudonym.

Writing a Cover Letter

A cover letter is a brief letter accompanying the submission of a manuscript. It introduces the manuscript and, if appropriate, you as well.

1. Always type your cover letter with a letter-quality typewriter, word processor, or printer.
2. Use either unlined white 8½″ × 11″ paper or your writer's business stationery. You may use stationery from your job only if it helps to establish your authority or expertise in the subject your piece is about. Do not use personal stationery.
3. Use a standard block or semiblock format.
4. Single-space; double-space between paragraphs.
5. Write to editors by name, or by name and title (for example, Jeanne Clark, Managing Editor), not merely by title.
6. Do not use Mr., Ms., Mrs., or Miss unless you are sure of the person's sex, marital status, and preference. Instead, write, "Dear Gayle Simon," etc.
7. Make your cover letter no longer than one page, except in highly unusual circumstances. It may be as short as two or three brief paragraphs.
8. Begin your cover letter by explaining what you're submitting. In your first paragraph, mention the title(s) and a few words of description: "six recent poems," "a first-person account of my year spent as a White House secretary," "a short story set in the mountains of Vermont," etc.
9. If the piece has appeared in print (or is scheduled for publication) elsewhere, explain when and where in your first paragraph.
10. If your manuscript has been written on speculation (see page 120 for details), or if the editor has specifically asked to see it (or your work in general), say so in paragraph one.
11. In your second paragraph, explain what makes your piece unusual, and/or what special experience you have had that informs it. If neither of these items applies (as will often be the case), omit this paragraph entirely.
12. In paragraph three, list your previous relevant sales and publications; if you have quite a few, stick with the major

ones. In either case, only mention the ones likely to impress the editor.

13. In this same paragraph, include any other *relevant* information about yourself and/or your writing—any significant writing awards or fellowships you've received, any significant and clearly related advanced study in writing, your previous publications on the same topic, etc.

14. If you have no publications or other achievements, omit paragraph three entirely.

15. Throughout your cover letter, stick to the facts. Don't compliment yourself or your piece. A cover letter is not an advertisement.

16. Do *not* mention any of the following in a cover letter:
    a. Who, if anyone, has read and rejected the piece.
    b. What anyone else has said about the piece. (You may, however, place a letter of endorsement from someone well-known after your cover letter.)
    c. How long and hard you've worked on the piece.
    d. Acknowledgment of others for their assistance.
    e. Any admission that the piece is in less than ideal shape. (If it still needs work, don't send it to editors yet!)
    f. A request for comments, criticism, advice, or instruction.
    g. How thrilled you would be to see your work in print.
    h. Anything about your life not strictly relevant to your submission.
    i. The rights you wish to sell.
    j. How much money you want for the piece (or any discussion of price or payment).
    k. Your social security number.
    l. Copyright information.

17. If you wish to make some positive comment about the publisher or publication (e.g., "I've been reading and enjoying *Yankee* for over a decade"), you may do so in a sentence or two toward the end of your letter. Be sincere; avoid overt flattery.

18. Your last paragraph should simply say, "I look forward to hearing from you. Please write or call if you have any questions."

19. Close with "Sincerely," "Cordially," or something similar.

20. Place your cover letter, face up, in the following spot:

a. If your manuscript is in a box: inside the box, on top of all other materials.
b. If your manuscript is in a two-pocket folder: clipped to the front of the folder, unfolded and face up.
c. If your manuscript is clipped together with a paper clip: inside the clip, on top of all other materials.
d. If your script (for TV, film, stage, etc.) is bound: clipped to the front cover or cover page.

If you are submitting more than one manuscript at once, clip your cover letter to the top manuscript or folder in the stack.

Submitting a Manuscript

Submit all manuscripts by mail or package delivery service (such as UPS). Do not use a fax or modem unless you have been specifically asked to do so.

Packing It Up

1. Keep your original; submit a good photocopy.
2. Put the following items together into each submission package: cover letter; manuscript(s); optional supporting materials (endorsements, photographs, etc.); return postage; return envelope or mailing bag.
3. If you are submitting a computer disc, attach a hard-copy cover letter to it. Do not submit a disc unless you have been asked to do so or are sure that the editor accepts disc submissions.
4. Package your work as follows:
   a. Very short work (six pages or less): folded in thirds, in a white #10 business envelope.
   b. Mid-length material: flat, in a 9″×12″ or 10″×13″ envelope.
   c. Large (boxed) manuscripts: in a padded mailing bag.
5. Enclose a sufficiently-large return envelope or mailing bag. Affix on it three typed mailing labels: two with your name and address (one for the destination address and one for the return address), and one with postal class instructions (First Class, Air Mail, etc.). Place it in the following location:
   a. #10 business envelope: folded in thirds, clipped behind

the last page of your manuscript.

    b. 9″ × 12″ or 10″ × 13″ envelope: folded in half, clipped behind the last page of your manuscript. (If you are using a two-pocket folder, place the envelope, unclipped, behind the manuscript in the right-hand pocket.)

    c. Mailing bag: flat, underneath your box or folder, unattached.

6. Also enclose return postage. With short manuscripts, slip it on top of your cover letter, under the paper clip. For manuscripts in boxes or two-pocket folders, place the postage in a #10 business envelope on which you have typed "Return Postage." Seal the envelope; place it just under your cover letter for a boxed manuscript, or in the left-hand pocket of your folder, on top of all other materials.

7. If you are submitting an unsolicited manuscript to a publisher outside of the country, enclose International Reply Coupons (of roughly equal value) instead of return postage. If you prefer, enclose only one IRC, and state in your cover letter that if your manuscript is rejected, you wish to receive nothing more than a letter of reply. IRCs are available at post offices.

8. Place everything carefully into your envelope or mailing bag. Affix three typed mailing labels to your package: one with the editor's name and address, one with your name and return address, and one with postal class instructions (First Class, Air Mail, etc.).

Mailing It Out

1. Mail manuscripts by first class or priority mail. Do not use book rate, parcel post, registered mail, certified mail, or third class. You may use private delivery services (UPS, Federal Express, etc.), but this probably won't impress anyone.

2. Do not purchase a return receipt unless you have good reason to believe that the publisher may not receive (or admit to receiving) your manuscript.

3. Send submissions to foreign countries via airmail—surface mail can take months. Some countries have special airmail rates for manuscripts; check at your post office.

4. Weigh your package carefully and determine the cost of postage. Enclose an equal amount of return postage (or the

equivalent in International Reply Coupons) inside your package.
5. Seal your package tightly. Reinforce your seal with transparent tape; staple shut all mailing bags.

Deciding Who, What, and Where
1. You may submit the same manuscript to as many different publishers as you wish at the same time. Exceptions: do not send the same piece simultaneously to two newspapers with largely overlapping readerships (e.g., the *Minneapolis Star Tribune* and the *St. Paul Pioneer Press*), or to more than one professional, technical, or scholarly journal.
2. Submit only one manuscript at a time to any one editor, with these exceptions:
   a. Submit short poems in groups of four to seven. Poems longer than about eight pages should be submitted on their own.
   b. Very short (1,500 words or less) prose pieces may be submitted singly or in groups of two or three.
   c. Very short books (such as the text for children's picture books) may be submitted singly, or in groups of two or three.
   d. Submit sample columns for syndication in groups of six to ten.
3. You may send an editor one manuscript, and then a second one a week or more later, even if they have not yet responded to the first. You may even send a third before you have received a reply to the first, but three is the limit.
4. You may send the same piece to two different editors at the same publication (but not simultaneously!), so long as they work independently (e.g., the lifestyles and Sunday supplement editors at the same newspaper).
5. Once your piece has been accepted and you have struck a deal, you must promptly withdraw it from consideration from any competitive publications. You need not withdraw it from publications that are willing to run reprints; but if one such publication offers to use your piece, you must mention the prior sale.

11 Things to Do When an Editor Is Slow to Respond

1. Wait the following amounts of time before inquiring about
    your unsolicited manuscript:
    a. Articles, essays, reviews, and short fiction: ten weeks.
    b. Poems: three months.
    c. Books: three months.
    d. Television, film, radio, stage, and video scripts: four
        months.
    If your manuscript was solicited, however, feel free to
    inquire after six weeks.
2. You may make your inquiry by phone or mail. Phoning,
    however, is quicker, easier, and much more likely to yield
    an answer.
3. If you do choose to inquire by mail, enclose a self-addressed,
    stamped envelope for a reply.
4. Your inquiry should be brief, businesslike, polite, and to the
    point. Mention your name, the title of the manuscript, and
    the date on which it was sent; then ask about its
    whereabouts.
5. If the proper person cannot or will not take your call, leave
    a message that includes your name, your phone number(s),
    the day and time of your call, and all the information in item
    4 above. Ask the editor to get back to you with an answer
    shortly.
6. If your call is not returned within three business days, call
    again. If your second call is not taken or returned in three
    more business days, write a brief letter, following the
    guidelines in steps 3 and 4 above.
7. If you receive no reply to your mail inquiry, assume you are
    being deliberately ignored, and send your manuscript
    elsewhere. However, do not withdraw your piece from
    consideration. There remains a slim chance that the editor
    will someday read it and offer to buy it.
8. If an editor tells you, "Your piece is here, but I'd like some
    more time to consider it," say okay, but add, "I'd like a
    response within the next two weeks." If necessary, follow
    up again after another month.
9. If an editor promises to check on your manuscript and get

back to you, but doesn't, call again a few days later. Follow steps 4 through 7 as necessary.

10. If an editor doesn't recall ever seeing your manuscript and can't find it, send a new copy.

11. If one submission to an editor disappears, it may still be worth trying that editor with another piece. If this happens twice, however, you should probably forget about that editor.

11 Tips on Writing a Query

A query *is a letter to an editor that describes a piece of writing and asks if the editor would like to see it. It is sent in lieu of an unsolicited manuscript.*

1. The most important rule about queries: *never* write one unless you have to.

2. Approach any editor you wish with an unsolicited freelance piece, even if notices in writers' books and magazines say not to. If and only if that piece is returned to you unread, with a note or form letter telling you that no unsolicited material will be considered (or if it is returned within a week with no note at all), should you write a query. You may direct your query to the very same editor who refused to read your unsolicited manuscript.

3. Queries are similar to cover letters in many ways, so follow tips 1-6 and 15-19 of "Writing a Cover Letter," on pages 111-113.

4. Keep queries for short manuscripts down to one page, except in unusual circumstances; queries for books may run as long as two pages.

5. Use your first one to four paragraphs to describe your piece in detail. If it is nonfiction, explain its theme, audience, approach, purpose, and overall content; also explain why the piece is important, unusual, or interesting. If the piece is fiction, write a very brief plot synopsis (four paragraphs maximum). Be sure to mention the piece's title.

6. In the following paragraph, list any previous sales and

publications likely to impress the editor. If you have quite a few, mention only the major ones.

7. In this same paragraph, include any other relevant information about yourself and your writing: any significant writing awards or fellowships you've received, any special experience you've had that informs your piece, etc. If you have no such experience, credentials, or sales, omit this paragraph.

8. In your next paragraph, ask the editor if they would like to see the manuscript ("This manuscript is ready for publication; would you care to see it?").

9. If you are querying about a book manuscript, you may (if you prefer) outline or synopsize its content in a separate document of two to seven pages, either 1½- or double-spaced. Omit any outline or synopsis from your cover letter, and simply say that an outline is attached.

10. Include a self-addressed, stamped #10 envelope for the editor's reply.

11. When an editor responds positively to your query, your piece has been **solicited**. Send it to that editor promptly, mentioning in your cover letter that you are sending the piece at their request. No return envelope or postage is necessary.

Getting Assignments

An assignment is a piece contracted for in advance and written to a set of specifications agreed upon by an editor and a writer.

Basic Facts on Assignments

1. Most nonfiction published in magazines, newspapers, and newsletters is written on assignment; so are many nonfiction books. Perhaps 20 percent of all published novels are written on assignment; short fiction, however, almost never is.

2. The idea for an assignment can come from you, an editor, someone else (such as the editor's boss), or some combination of these people.

3. The smaller a publication is (and/or the lower its rates of

payment), the easier it is to get an assignment from its editor. You must have significant credentials and experience to get an assignment from a major magazine; however, it is often possible to get an assignment from a small-town or neighborhood newspaper simply by asking for one and demonstrating decent writing skills.

4. You must make a clear written or oral agreement with your editor before you begin writing; this agreement should cover when and how much you'll be paid, the length of your piece, your delivery date, provisions for doing a rewrite if the editor thinks the piece needs it, and the size of the kill fee (to be paid if the piece is unusable). For details, see "11 Key Points of an Assignment Agreement" on pages 177-178.

5. Expect (and insist on) a written contract for any freelance magazine assignment, unless the publication is very small or pays in copies. Oral contracts are the norm for newspapers and newsletters, however.

6. When you write a piece on assignment, you are obligated to follow your agreed-upon guidelines and turn in the piece by your deadline. If the piece is suitable, your editor is obligated to pay you in full for it; however, they are *not* legally obligated to publish it.

7. If you miss your deadline, your editor is no longer obligated to accept and pay for your piece, and you are not entitled to a kill fee. However, the editor may choose to accept and pay for your piece anyway. If your piece is refused, you may, of course, sell it elsewhere.

8. If your editor does not consider your piece publishable as written, they must give you specific suggestions for revisions (and a reasonable deadline for doing them) or a kill fee, which scratches the whole deal. If you do a rewrite at the editor's request, and they also find the rewrite unacceptable, they will pay you your kill fee, cancelling the assignment. All rights to the piece then revert to you. (Publishers and publications that pay in copies do not pay kill fees.)

9. If you are asked to do a rewrite, you have the right to cancel the assignment, forfeit your payment, accept a kill fee, and take your piece elsewhere. (You won't get any further assignments from that editor, of course.)

10. Selling a book based on a proposal is a form of writing on assignment. You essentially sell your idea and your writing

ability; only after signing a contract do you complete the book. However, with a book you usually get some money up front, which is not normally the case with magazine and newspaper assignments.

11. In most cases, ask for an assignment by letter. In the case of a very small publication (such as a small-town or neighborhood newspaper, or another local publication), you may make your pitch in person. Call the publisher or editor to set up an appointment; bring writing samples to the appointment with you.

12. Sometimes editors respond to assignment requests by asking writers to do pieces **on speculation** or **on spec**. This means the editor is interested in the piece and the writer, but is unwilling to make a commitment of any kind. In other words, they are soliciting a manuscript that has not yet been written. No oral or written agreement is necessary or appropriate for a spec piece.

Writing an Assignment Query

1. You may approach editors for assignments in either of two ways: by suggesting an idea of your own, or by offering to write one or more assignments based on the editor's own ideas.

2. To get any assignment, you must be able to convince an editor of your ability as a writer. If you are suggesting your own idea for a piece, you must also convince the editor that your piece will be worth publishing.

3. Your letter should be no more than two pages; one page is typical.

4. Assignment queries follow many of the same rules as cover letters, so follow tips 1-6 and 15-19 from "Writing a Cover Letter," on pages 111-113.

5. If you are suggesting a specific piece or idea, spend your first two to four paragraphs outlining it. Explain who it is for, what it will do (instruct, inform, provide basic background), and what makes it useful or interesting to the publication's readers. Suggest a specific length. If you are not suggesting a specific piece or idea, skip these paragraphs.

6. Spend two to four paragraphs introducing yourself, your writing experience, your sales and publications, your expertise in the subject, and/or any other relevant

credentials. Focus on those items most likely to impress the editor. Specifically mention other publications you've written for on assignment, if any.

7. Include photocopies of two or three of your previously published short pieces (sometimes called **clippings**); mention in your letter that you're enclosing them. These samples should be as closely related to your suggested topic and to the publication you are contacting as possible. Ideally, at least one of the samples should have been written on assignment; if it was, say so in your letter. (Unpublished pieces are better than nothing, but are far less impressive than published work.) If it's important that these samples be returned, say so.

8. If you're suggesting a specific piece or idea, your next paragraph should explain that you'd like to write this piece on assignment; if you're interested in assignments in general, simply say that you'd like to do some freelance work on assignment.

9. Close this paragraph with *a few* positive words about your ability and work habits (e.g., "I work fast, am scrupulous about meeting deadlines, and do thorough research."). Be truthful and factual; don't advertise or flatter yourself (e.g., "I do first-rate work and have a jazzy style.").

10. In your next paragraph, request a response from the editor. For example, "If this prospect interests you, please get in touch. I'd be happy to discuss this project (or other writing assignments) with you."

11. Enclose a self-addressed, stamped envelope for the editor's response. Make sure it is large enough (and has sufficient postage) for the return of your work samples.

12. When submitting a book proposal, you need not write a full-fledged assignment query. Simply write a cover letter, following the guidelines on pages 111-113, and send it with your proposal.

13. If you have two good ideas that might be suitable for the same editor or publication, you may suggest both assignments in a single letter of no more than two pages. Two ideas at once is the maximum, however.

14. If you receive no response to your assignment query within one month, make a polite follow-up call; if necessary, call

again a week later. If the editor neither takes nor returns either call, forget about that editor.

15. If an editor turns down an assignment idea but does not seem unwilling to work with you, feel free to try again with another assignment suggestion.

Handling Deadlines

1. Set deadlines you can reasonably meet—not ones you hope you can meet or ones you can meet only if everything goes smoothly.

2. Always build in a buffer—ask for 25 to 35 percent more time than you think you will need. This will allow for snags, family emergencies, or distractions.

3. If an editor tries to set an unreasonable deadline, *don't accept it*. Insist on a deadline you can actually meet. If you agree to an impossible deadline, *you* will be the one blamed if you miss it. It's better to pass up an impossible assignment than to accept it and fail.

4. Once you've agreed to a deadline, meet it.

5. If it looks like you are probably going to miss a deadline, see if there's a different way to handle your piece so that you can finish it sooner. Can you change your approach, your structure, or your degree of depth or detail?

6. If you realize that you will not be able to meet a deadline *for any reason*, let your editor know *immediately*. Name a date by which you reasonably believe you *can* finish the piece. The sooner an editor knows you'll be late, the smaller your chances of losing the assignment.

7. If you are late turning in an assignment, your editor has the legal right to not use it, not pay you for it, and not pay you a kill fee—unless the editor has agreed to extend your deadline.

8. Deadlines for newspapers are the most urgent and least flexible; those for books are typically the least urgent and most flexible. Magazines fall midway in between.

9. The more you meet or beat deadlines, the more you build your reputation, and the more editors will want to keep working with you.

24 Tips on Asking for More Money

1. You always have the right to ask any editor or publisher for more money, and to take your piece elsewhere if the editor says no.

2. Similarly, every editor or publisher has the right to say, "I can't (or won't) offer a penny more. Accept my offer or take your piece elsewhere." An editor who says this obviously risks losing the chance to publish your piece.

3. No sane editor will ever scuttle a deal just because you asked for more money. At worst the editor will stick to the original offer—which you can then accept if you wish.

4. *Never* announce in a cover letter how much money you want or expect to get for a piece. Do not bring up the topic of money until an editor offers to publish it.

5. Keep in mind that most editors can be at least a little bit flexible about money.

6. Normally your editor or publisher will quote you a price they'd like to pay; you may then say yes, say no, or ask for more.

7. You may ask for more money by either mail or phone, but the phone is usually quicker and easier.

8. Present your desire for more money as a statement rather than a question. Don't say, "Could I have $200 more?" Instead, say, "Go to $500 and we've got a deal," or "I need $500 for this piece," or "$300 is too low, but $500 is okay."

9. Consider the size and the normal rates of the particular publisher or publication. If a major women's magazine were to offer you $300 for your 2,000-word article, you should ask for more money, because it can surely afford more (and normally pays more). But if the *St. Paul Pioneer Press* (a mid-size daily newspaper) were to offer you that same amount for your piece, take it—it's both fair and in line with what that paper typically pays.

10. On rare occasions, you may be asked, "How much money are you looking for?" Respond by asking for an amount that is on the high end of reasonable *for that publisher or publication.*

11. The more previous sales and publications you have, and/or the wider reputation you have as an authority on your

subject, the more likely editors are to agree to a request for more money.

12. The more material you've published, and/or the more work you've sold to that editor before, the more money you should be getting per word, per page, or per line. The first time an editor accepts one of your pieces, you may be offered the publication's lowest rate of payment. By your third or fourth sale to that editor, however, you should be getting a higher rate—and that rate should go up with every third or fourth sale thereafter. If you're not offered more, ask for it.

13. Consider the value of compromise. If an editor offers you $500, you ask for $800, and your editor says, "Let's split the difference," consider the offer very seriously. If the editor responds, "I just can't go that high," then *you* can suggest splitting the difference.

14. Sometimes it's wise to ask for more than you want, need, or expect, so that your editor can make a counteroffer that's close to what you hoped for. As before, ask for an amount that's on the high end of reasonable.

15. Feel free to dicker. If you ask for $200 more and your editor says, "I can go $50 higher, but not $200," ask for $75 or $100 more instead.

16. Also feel free to trade terms for money, or vice versa. For example, you might agree to do a piece for the editor's price of $300, but at two-thirds the length they suggested. Or you might insist on an advance that's $2,000 higher, but agree to be paid that last $2,000 six months from now instead of immediately.

17. Trust your hunches and instincts. There are few absolute rules about asking for more money; you'll usually have to feel your way as you negotiate. You'll get better at this with experience.

18. Keep in mind that a few publications—particularly some literary magazines—pay set, nonnegotiable rates for material. If an editor tells you, "Sorry, that's our standard rate, and I can't change it," they are usually telling the truth.

19. If an editor or publisher doesn't offer you any money at all for your piece (or any advance for your book), feel free to ask for money up front. (The exceptions are publications that have never paid their writers any money and clearly

never will: scholarly journals, neighborhood newspapers, church newsletters, etc.)

20. Once you and your editor or publisher have agreed, either orally or in writing, on the sum you are to receive for your piece, that agreement is legally binding and cannot (except under truly extraordinary circumstances) be changed — so don't try to.
21. You do not always have to ask for more money. If the payment you are offered seems fair, reasonable, and appropriate, feel free to take it without dickering.
22. Remember that in publishing (and in life), it is often true that you don't get something unless you ask for it.
23. See chapter eleven of this book for extensive information on contracts and contract negotiation.
24. For still more detailed information on negotiating a publishing contract, consult one or more of these books:
    a. *A Writer's Guide to Contract Negotiations* by Richard Balkin (Writer's Digest Books)
    b. *The Indispensable Writer's Guide* by Scott Edelstein (HarperCollins)
    c. *Negotiating a Book Contract* by Mark L. Levine (Moyer Bell)

12 Tips on Using the Phone

1. Never be afraid to use the phone to contact anyone in publishing.
2. Don't expect that everyone you call will be willing to speak with you, however.
3. *Do* expect anyone with whom you have a working relationship to take and return your calls.
4. Use the phone whenever it will save time or effort for you or the person you're calling. When a letter will be faster, more convenient, or more efficient, write instead.
5. Be polite, straightforward, and businesslike at all times. Do not get chatty unless someone clearly invites you to.
6. Be respectful of other people's time; make your calls as brief as you can — without hurrying or being rude, or course. If you believe a call will take more than a few minutes, say so at the beginning.
7. Begin each call by identifying yourself and explaining your

reason for calling. Then ask, "Can you talk for a minute?" or "Is now a good time to talk?" If the answer is no, set up an alternate time to call back or receive a call.

8. If the person you're calling can't or won't take your call, leave a message that includes your name, your phone number(s), the day and time of your call, *and your reason for calling*.

9. If you leave a message and your call is not returned within three business days, try again. If this call is not taken or returned after three more business days, write a letter. If you receive no response to your letter within three weeks, either give up or contact the person's superior.

10. Pay for all long-distance calls yourself, with these exceptions:
    a. If you are calling a publishing firm at the request of someone at that firm, you may make the call collect, person-to-person.
    b. If you are writing a piece on assignment, and your editor has agreed in advance to pay for any related long-distance calls, pay for the calls yourself and submit a copy of your itemized phone bill (with the relevant calls highlighted) when it arrives. Ask and expect to be reimbursed within thirty days.

11. Whenever you discuss anything important over the phone, take notes—and hang onto them. If you make an oral agreement regarding publication of your work, type up your notes promptly and send them to your editor, to make sure both of you are clear about your agreement.

12. If something is important enough, put it in writing.

Correcting Galleys and Page Proofs

*Just before your piece goes to press, you may be sent either **page proofs** (typeset text, formatted into pages) or **galleys** (strips of typeset text, not yet formatted) to be examined, corrected, and returned. Here are some tips that will help.*

1. Virtually every book publisher, and about half of all

magazines, supply authors with page proofs or galleys. Newspapers, however, almost never do.

2. Read all galleys and page proofs extremely carefully, with the goal of catching every error of every kind.
3. Compare the proofs or galleys carefully against your original manuscript, so that you can easily detect any change or omission.
4. Use the proofreader's marks described on pages 26-28 to make corrections and changes.
5. If an editor has made any significant addition, omission, or change that you object to, call them immediately to discuss it.
6. Check any information that may have changed since you first wrote the piece—particularly names, titles, phone numbers, and addresses. Update them in your text as necessary.
7. Return the page proofs or galleys by the deadline set by your publisher. If they arrive late, some or all of your corrections may not get incorporated into the final printed text.

11 Good Ways to Get Along With Editors

1. Be reasonable, polite, straightforward, and businesslike at all times.
2. Do whatever you say you'll do, and don't agree to do anything you can't.
3. Be assertive. Ask for what you want or need. Stand up for yourself when necessary.
4. Cut editors a little slack, but not a lot. Be flexible and understanding, but speak out firmly whenever you feel you're not being treated fairly.
5. Hold editors accountable for whatever they do, but don't blame them for other people's errors.
6. Correct galleys and page proofs carefully and thoroughly, and return them on time.
7. Do your best to meet or beat all deadlines.
8. Try to work with, rather than against, your editor on matters of editing and rewriting.
9. When your editor does you a favor or does a good job, express your appreciation.

10. Whenever a problem does arise, bring it up with your editor promptly, straightforwardly, and calmly.
11. Write the very best work that you can.

The Fast Track to Success

If you want to build your writing career in a hurry, and are willing and able to write primarily or solely nonfiction, follow these steps:

1. Approach the editor of a small-town newspaper, a surburban newspaper, or a neighborhood publication. Offer to do some freelance pieces on whatever topics the editor desires, on speculation.
2. Keep approaching the editors of such publications until at least one accepts your offer.
3. Write for this editor until he or she accepts one of your pieces. You may do this for more than one publication at a time.
4. Continue writing for this publication until you've published ten or more pieces. Save copies of published pieces to use as clippings.
5. Approach the editors of larger publications in your area, such as the Sunday supplement of the nearest big-city paper, your weekly independent arts and entertainment paper, or the local or regional slick full-color monthly. Either send in ideas for assignments or ask to be given an assignment of the editor's choice. Enclose photocopies ("clippings") of your previous publications. If necessary, offer to do a piece on spec.
6. Continue writing for these publications until you've published five or more pieces in them.
7. Write and submit some finished pieces to national publications focusing on specific subjects (such as sailing, single parenting, massage, tropical fish, or crafts). If you prefer, suggest some assignment ideas to their editors.
8. Keep writing for national special-interest publications until you've sold a total of five or six pieces to at least two different magazines.

9. Write a proposal for a nonfiction book using the guidelines on pages 60-63 of this volume.
10. If the proposal is highly specialized, market it yourself using the tips in chapters six and seven. If it has a large potential readership, contact some agents using the suggestions in chapter nine, and arrange to have one represent the project.
11. Once the proposal sells, write the best book you can.
12. Write and market another nonfiction book proposal, and another.
13. As you write, keep your eyes open for other opportunities (lecturing, ghostwriting, documentary scripting, etc.). When good ones come along, grab them.
14. Watch the momentum build.

Writing Spinoffs

A *spinoff is a new variation on a previously-written piece that reaches a different audience, takes a different approach, or has a different slant or focus.*

1. Almost any good idea can lend itself to several different variations. Spinoffs enable you to make the most (and the most money) out of any strong concept.
2. Writing a spinoff usually requires little extra time or research; it's simply a matter of presenting the same concept, information, or insight in a different way.
3. Every spinoff is considered a new piece. This means that you can sell first rights to each new variation on your basic theme, and earn first rights money from each sale.
4. Here are some ways to generate spinoff projects:
   a. Narrow, widen, or change your audience (e.g., from working mothers to working fathers).
   b. Narrow, widen, or change your topic (e.g., from breakthroughs in transplant surgery to breakthroughs in kidney transplants).
   c. Stick with your topic, but change your structure (e.g., from an overview to a how-to piece).
   d. Stick with your structure, but change your topic (e.g., after you've sold "The 10 Best Office Products," write

"The 10 Best Kitchen Products").

    e. Write a sequel (e.g., "10 More of the Best Office Products" or "The 10 Worst Office Products").

    f. In fiction, write the further adventures of a character or group of characters; or tell the same story from a different character's point of view; or write another piece set in the same place.

5. Spinoffs must be marketed carefully. You'll need to find a publisher or publication that targets the same audience as your spinoff.

6. Mention in your cover letter where your previous pieces on the same topic—including any previous spinoffs—have been published. This helps to establish your expertise in (or at least familiarity with) the subject.

7. After you've sold first rights to your original piece, and to any spinoffs, you can then sell reprint and foreign rights to each one.

8
Selling Yourself and Your Services

✔

✔

✔

43 Professional Opportunities for Writers

Below is a list of many jobs that use writing, editing, and other literary skills.

1. Journalist
2. Staff writer
3. Editor (includes a variety of positions, such as managing editor, copy editor, acquisitions editor, production editor, assistant editor, etc.)
4. Technical writer/editor
5. Proofreader
6. Manuscript reader/evaluator (for a publisher)
7. Editorial assistant/editorial secretary
8. Copy clerk/editorial aide (halfway between a gofer and an editorial assistant)
9. Copy writer (for catalogs, instruction manuals, etc.)
10. Script writer/editor for TV, film, radio, etc.
11. Business script writer (writing audio, video, and/or AV scripts for business, industry, nonprofits, etc.)
12. Public relations/communications writer/director
13. Advertising writer
14. Publicist/publicity writer
15. Literary agent
16. Agent's assistant
17. Publisher
18. Publisher's assistant
19. Columnist (local or syndicated)
20. Reviewer (of books, art, film, food, etc.)
21. Gag writer (for cartoonists or comedians)
22. Speechwriter
23. Résumé writer
24. Grant writer
25. Ghostwriter
26. Researcher/fact-checker
27. Translator
28. Indexer
29. Writing consultant
30. Writer-in-residence
31. Storyteller

32. Writing tutor
33. High school English teacher
34. College writing and/or literature instructor
35. Freelance writing teacher (through community education programs, writers' workshops, and similar programs)
36. English-as-a-foreign-language instructor (teaching English in a foreign country)
37. English-as-a-second-language instructor
38. Reading teacher/tutor (in schools and literacy programs)
39. Publishing employee (in subsidiary rights, promotion, design, etc.)
40. Anthology editor
41. Lecturer/speaker
42. Librarian
43. Bookstore manager

20 People and Organizations That Hire Writers

1. Publishers of all types
2. Technical writing/editing firms
3. Editorial consulting firms
4. Literary centers
5. Book packagers
6. Colleges and universities (as writing instructors and public relations people)
7. Advertising agencies
8. Public relations and publicity agencies
9. Government agencies and departments—on the federal, state, provincial, county, and city level
10. Hospitals and other large health care organizations
11. National associations, unions, and professional organizations
12. National headquarters for most religious, political, scholarly, consumer, technical, scientific, and other special-interest organizations
13. Most large nonprofit organizations
14. Any organization that communicates with its members and/or employees through a newspaper, a newsletter, or internal news releases (including most large organizations)
15. Any organization that must communicate with the outside,

through news releases, brochures, manuals, catalogs, instructions, and/or publicity pieces (including virtually every organization with over a hundred employees)
16. Business people, politicians, and government officials who must make frequent speeches
17. People with good ideas for written works who lack the skill or time to write those pieces on their own
18. People who need to promote or advertise themselves, their skills, their products, or their services
19. Other writers with manuscripts that need critiquing, editing, rewriting, or ghostwriting
20. Experts who have important information to impart to others but not the ability or time to do the necessary writing on their own

Creating Your Own Writing Opportunities

Many writers have built writing careers by clearing their own paths rather than following existing ones. Here are some options to consider for your own career:

1. Propose a new column or regular feature to a publication you enjoy and feel qualified to write for.
2. Sell a new writing-related service (personalized greeting cards, limericks to go, personalized answering-machine messages, on-premises editing at a local print shop, etc.) to individuals and/or organizations.
3. Sell your services as a part- or full-time writer-in-residence to public and private schools, community service organizations, and other institutions. As a writer-in-residence, you might teach classes, visit other teachers' classes, teach in-service workshops, critique people's work, do writing to order for the organization, give readings and talks, and/or generally be available as a resource.
4. Sell a new product that uses your writing skills. Market it through retail outlets, by mail, or both. Todd Strasser successfully marketed Dr. Wing Tip Shoo's X-Rated Fortune Cookies in this manner.
5. Self-publish your own book(s), and market and promote

it/them like crazy. See "Tips on Self-Promotion" below and "13 Tips on Self-Publishing" on pages 74-75, for details.
6. Start your own newsletter or magazine — one that reaches an audience that has thus far gone unaddressed.
7. Come up with something so new and original that it doesn't fit any of the six categories above.

Finding Your Niche(s)

One of the best and fastest ways to build a writing career — and to sell your work, talents, and services — is to find (or create) a niche and fill it. Better yet, find and fill several. To find or create your own niches, ask yourself the following questions:

1. What can I do that no one else can?
2. What do I know or understand that no one else knows?
3. What have I experienced that few others have?
4. What ideas do I have that are new or unique?
5. What perspectives do I have that are special or different? What do I see that others do not?
6. What does the world (country, state, city, suburb, neighborhood, industry, etc.) need that I can offer?
7. What seems to be missing that I can provide? What have other writers overlooked?

Tips on Self-Promotion

General Tips
1. Don't be afraid to promote yourself and your work. Self-promotion is an important part of building and maintaining a writing career.
2. Always keep in mind that your goals are to increase your visibility, build your career, and achieve success — not to massage your ego. Don't use self-promotion just to flatter yourself.
3. For excellent and detailed information on self-promotion, consult these books:

a. *Publicity for Books and Authors* by Peggy Glenn (Aames-Allen)
b. *The Unabashed Self-Promoter's Guide* by Jeffrey Lant (JLA Publications)
c. *The Writer's Guide to Self-Promotion and Publicity* by Elaine Feldman (Writer's Digest Books)

Guidelines for Promoting Yourself

1. Give readings of your work (especially when you have just published a new book); if possible, arrange a multicity reading tour. See "Arranging Readings" on pages 144-146 for details.

2. Do book signings, both in your home town and elsewhere. See "Arranging Book Signings" on pages 147-149 for details.

3. If you have expertise or experience worth communicating to others, arrange lecturing and speaking gigs, either on your own or through a lecture agent.

4. Have business cards printed up. Give one to anyone who might conceivably use your services or be able to help you, including every editor or producer who has accepted your work or given you an assignment.

5. When your new book is published or your new script is performed or aired, throw a publication or production party. Invite friends, other writers, people you know in the industry, and people you would like to meet.

6. Send out copies of your new book to reviewers, editors (both those you have worked with and those you hope to), and anyone else you think might be able to help you.

7. Seek endorsements of your work from well-known writers and other personalities. (Some writers do this by sending out pre-publication galleys of their books.)

8. Promote yourself to the media as someone worth interviewing and writing (or talking) about. Send out press releases. Make up and send out press packets to magazines, newspapers, and television and radio stations. (Radio stations are particularly interested in interviewing writers, usually via phone.) See the books noted above (particularly *Publicity for Books and Authors*) for details on preparing press releases and press kits.

9. Publish your book(s) yourself. See "13 Tips on Self-Publishing" on pages 74-75 for details.
10. *Never* push your friends or family to help you in your promotional efforts, or even to buy or see your work. This isn't fair to the other people, and it can strain your relationship with them. Do feel free to *invite* people to events and performances, and to accept their help if they offer it freely.

Composing a Writer's Résumé

1. Write your own résumé; don't hire someone else to do it for you.
2. Consider your résumé as both a summary of your credentials and experience *and* a sample of your clearest, most concise writing.
3. Use a *letter-quality* printer or typewriter and a clear, easy-to-read typeface. Laser-jet printing is nice but not necessary.
4. Avoid fancying up your résumé with photographs, borders, or illustrations. Keep it simple and straightforward.
5. Use a good-quality paper (such as linen, cotton, or classic laid) in white or an unobtrusive color (beige, tan, light gray, very light blue, or buff).
6. Single- or 1½-space text. Double-, 2½-, or triple-space between sections.
7. Organize your résumé in a format that is neat, attractive, visually appealing, and easy to read and scan. A two-column format usually works best.
8. Make your résumé no less than one page and no more than two.
9. Do not try to be as detailed as possible (unless you have few credentials and little experience). Your goal is to communicate your skills and experience as quickly, clearly, and succinctly as possible.
10. Do not put the word "résumé" at the top of your first page; begin with your name, address, and phone number(s). Include all phone numbers where you can be easily reached.
11. Omit any information not directly pertaining to the position you are seeking. Do not mention your age, marital status, hobbies, or social security number.

12. Most résumés get no more than a one-minute scan, so make yours as easily-scannable as possible:
    a. Separate your résumé into several clearly-defined categories (e.g., Publications, Articles, Books, Scripts, Work for Hire, Education, Ghostwriting, Editing, Reviewing, Reporting, Past Clients, Awards, Consulting, Teaching, etc.).
    b. Use bulleted lists (of clients, publications, duties, skills, etc.). Avoid paragraphs of description or narration.
    c. Underline key words and phrases (or use bold face or all capitals) to add emphasis and visual contrast.
    d. Leave plenty of white space to provide visual breaks.
13. Present the different categories of information in whatever order makes you look best *for the particular position you are seeking*. If you are hoping to land a job ghostwriting a book, list your books and previous ghostwriting experience first; if you are applying for a job as a newspaper arts editor, list your reviewing and journalism experience first.
14. You may list items within each category in any of the following orders:
    a. Reverse chronological. (This is standard.)
    b. Chronological. (Not recommended; this usually lists your most significant credentials last and the least significant ones first.)
    c. In order of significance, with the most significant first.
15. When citing dates, use years only. One exception: when citing specific issues of magazines or newspapers, list complete issue dates.
16. Your résumé should make you look as close to ideally qualified as possible for whatever position you are seeking. This means that you will need to tailor a different résumé for each type of position—in some cases, for each different job. If you have a computer or word processor, tailor and print out a separate résumé for each job you qualify for. If you just have a typewriter, type up all the different possible sections of your résumé on individual pages. For each job, pick out the appropriate sections and arrange them in the order that makes you look best; then assemble a résumé for photocopying using scissors and tape.
17. List professional (but not personal) references as the final section of your résumé—or, if you prefer, list them on a

separate page as an attachment. Your résumé and references should add up to no more than three pages.

18. Place your name on the top of page two of your résumé, and on top of your references page. Also indicate a page number on the top of page two.

19. Triple-check your spelling, grammar, and punctuation; also check each detail for accuracy. Remember that your résumé is an indication of your neatness, attention to detail, and ability to write clear, correct, concise English.

20. If you are applying for a college teaching job, refer to your résumé as a c.v. (curriculum vita).

Preparing Invoices

Use an invoice whenever you turn in a manuscript written on assignment. Also use one to bill a person or organization for your services.

General Tips on Invoices

1. Use your writer's business stationery or plain $8\frac{1}{2}" \times 11"$ paper on which you have typed your name, address, and phone number at the top.

2. Type the entire invoice using a letter-quality typewriter, word processor, or printer. Single-space; double-space between items.

3. Submit one copy of each invoice to the person who gave you the assignment or contracted for your services; if the person has left the organization, send the invoice to their successor. Keep a copy in your files (or stored on a disc).

4. A few lines down from your phone number, type the current date. Two lines below the date, type "Invoice" in bold face or all capitals.

5. Two lines down, type "Client:"; on the next few lines, type the name and job title of your contact; the name of the publisher, publication, or organization they work for; and the billing address.

6. If you are being reimbursed for any expenses (travel, long-distance phone charges, etc.), include these as separate line items under the heading "Reimbursable Expenses." Note each amount and what each charge is for. Also indicate a

subtotal for all such charges on a separate line. Attach copies of any phone bills, receipts, etc.

7. Near the bottom of the invoice, type "Total Amount Due: $_____" in all capitals or bold face, with the proper amount filled in.

8. Two lines below, type in bold face or all capitals, "Please pay within thirty days."

9. If you do not receive full payment within thirty days, send a second invoice, identical to the first, with these exceptions:

    a. Place the current date at the top.

    b. Two lines below the date, type in all capitals or bold face: "Second Notice—Past Due Amount."

    c. If you have received partial payment, indicate this as a credit and adjust the total amount due accordingly.

If full payment hasn't arrived within a month after sending this second notice, call to politely but firmly discuss the problem.

Invoices for Assignments

1. Two lines beneath client information, type "Re:" and the title of the piece you are turning in.

2. Drop down two lines; type "Description:" and a brief description (five to twelve words) of the piece, including the approximate word-length.

3. Drop down two more lines: type "Delivery date:" and the date you are mailing the assignment.

4. Two lines below, type "Payment due: _____, as per our agreement of _____." Fill in the appropriate amount and date.

5. You may list more than one item (e.g., two different pieces, or text and photography) on one invoice. List the amount due for each as well as a total amount due at the bottom.

6. Enclose the invoice with your piece, between your letter and your manuscript.

Invoices for Services

1. Two lines beneath client information, type "Billing period: _____." Fill in the month or days that make up the billing period.

2. Drop down two lines and type "Services provided:"

Directly beneath this, one item per line, offer a breakdown of everything you've done for the client during the billing period, plus the number of hours spent at each task. Example:

Preparation of author biography	1.5 hours
Telephone consultation	.5 hours

If your list has only one item, that's okay.

3. At the end of this list, type "Total hours: _____." Fill in the total; double-check your addition.
4. Drop down two more lines. Type "Rate: _____/hr." Fill in your hourly charge.
5. If you are being paid by the page or some other measure, replace the hourly rate with this rate. If you are being paid a flat rate for your services, omit any mention of rates or hours. Instead, simply type, "Payment due: _____, as per our agreement of _____." Fill in the appropriate amount and date.

11 Useful Accoutrements

1. Business cards. Inexpensive and extremely helpful for self-promotion.
2. A telephone answering machine. Enables editors and other important people to reach you by phone at any time.
3. Call waiting. Enables you to take two calls on a single phone at once.
4. A tape recorder. Essential for interviews.
5. Business stationery (letterhead and envelopes). Very important for looking professional to businesses, nonprofit organizations, and other people and organizations to which you hope to sell your services. Matching mailing labels are also very useful.
6. Return address labels for correspondence. Buy attractive (but not glitzy) ones.
7. A briefcase. Essential when you're selling yourself or your services in person.
8. A photocopier. Convenient but expensive.
9. A modem. For downloading text directly into a publisher's computer.
10. A fax or computer fax board. Fax machines are becoming

more and more widely used—and they double as photocopiers.
11. A rolodex. Provides quick, easy access for addresses and phone numbers.

10 Tips on Ghostwriting

1. **Ghostwriting** can refer to any of the following arrangements:
   a. You write a piece, but someone else is credited as the author.
   b. You write a piece in collaboration with someone, but receive no byline.
   c. You share a byline with someone else, but in fact do all (or the vast majority) of the writing.
   d. You write a piece (usually a genre novel) under a "house name": a pseudonym used for all the pieces in the series.
2. Ghostwriters are hired by the following people and organizations:
   a. Writers who need help with projects
   b. Publishers
   c. Literary agents
   d. Book packagers
   e. Editorial services
   f. Celebrities, such as politicians, athletes, and actors and actresses. (More often than not, publishers hire ghostwriters for celebrities, but some celebrities do their own hiring.)
   g. Government officials, presidents of corporations and nonprofit organizations, and other people who give frequent speeches.
3. Always sign a written agreement *in advance* for any ghostwriting deal; if necessary, draw up the agreement yourself. This agreement should address the following issues:
   a. How much you are to be paid, and when.
   b. Your responsibilities as a ghostwriter, including the estimated length of the project and your deadline for completing it.
   c. Whether you will receive a byline, and if so, how the byline will appear (your name first, your name second,

"with" instead of "and" before your name, etc.).
   d. The other person's responsibilities (to give you notes or
      a first draft, to be regularly available for interviews, to
      provide personal papers, etc.).
For your protection, specify all of the above in writing—
unless the ghostwriting project is a part of your duties as a
regular employee, in which case no written agreement is
necessary.

4. Ghostwriting contracts, like most other agreements, are
   negotiable—often considerably so.
5. Payment for ghostwriting differs widely from project to
   project. Here are some options:
   a. Payment of a flat fee on completion of the project (or
      two or more smaller fees, each paid on completion of a
      portion of the project).
   b. Payment of an hourly fee for your work. This may be
      paid at the completion of the project or in installments
      as the project proceeds.
   c. A percentage of all the money the project earns. (This
      varies from 25 to 60 percent.) This option is worthwhile
      only if the project already has a publisher, and if you are
      guaranteed a specific dollar amount from the advance.
   d. Payment of an initial fee, plus a percentage of whatever
      the project earns beyond the advance. (This is common
      for book projects.)
6. Never agree to ghostwrite a project on spec—that is, to write
   it and be paid a percentage of the money it earns *only if it
   sells*. This is a prescription for disaster, since most such
   projects do not sell. Insist on at least a flat fee up front.
7. Ghostwriters generally earn between $25 and $60 an hour,
   plus potential royalties in many cases.
8. Be careful about whom you work with. People who hire (or
   need) ghostwriters are often egocentric, absurdly busy,
   unavailable, or outright unbalanced. Don't agree to work
   with someone you doubt you'll be able to get along with—
   or, worse, with someone who will make your task
   impossible.
9. Ghostwriting gigs are hard to get (most are set up via
   referrals and networking), and they require extensive
   writing experience in the appropriate genre. However, if
   you have the necessary experience, you may be able to sell

your services as a ghostwriter to some of the following people and organizations:

   a. Book packagers (see the heading "Book Producers" in the reference work *Literary Market Place* for a list of these)
   b. Editorial services (see the heading of the same name in *Literary Market Place*)
   c. Your agent
   d. Any book publisher that has accepted at least one of your books
10. If at any point you realize that a ghostwriting project is not going to work out, say so, and back out as gracefully and quickly as possible.

Arranging Readings

Arranging public readings of your prose or poetry is not difficult. Unless you only write essays, it is not usually necessary to have been extensively published—or even published at all. What is necessary is that you have completed work that is good enough and polished enough to present before an audience.

Organizations That Frequently Sponsor Readings
1. Writers' centers
2. Bookstores
3. College and universities (through their English and Creative Writing departments, their student activities boards, and/or student organizations—e.g., the Newman Center or the black student association).
4. Cafes, coffee houses, and bars
5. Libraries
6. Art centers
7. Literary festivals
8. Writers' clubs and other writers' organizations
9. Writers' conferences and workshops
10. Arts councils

Organizations That Occasionally Sponsor Readings
1. Community and cultural centers
2. Churches, synagogues, and other religious groups and organizations
3. Public and private high schools
4. Women's centers
5. Theaters
6. Museums and art galleries
7. Community service organizations (public interest groups, nature centers, city recreation departments, YMCAs and YWCAs, senior citizens' centers, etc.)
8. Public radio stations

Organizing a Reading
1. You may apply to read your work through an established reading series or set up a reading on your own—or both.
2. If you wish to read your work through an established reading series, call the sponsoring organization to ask about its standard procedure for giving (or applying to give) a reading. Most reading series are competitive, based on the submission of a sample of your work; if you are selected, however, you need not read the same piece or pieces you submitted for evaluation. Payment ranges from $10 to $150; $50 to $100 is typical.
3. To organize a reading on your own, contact the program director at each of the above organizations that interests you. If you offer to give a reading at no charge, you will sharply increase your chances of getting a positive response. Another option is to agree to split the admission fees with the sponsoring organization. (About half of all readings are free; most others, except those given by well-known writers, cost $3 or less for admission.) You can also, of course, sponsor your own reading by renting a space and doing your own publicity.
4. Don't flood your market. Limit your readings in any metropolitan area to two a year. (In very large metro areas—San Francisco, New York, Dallas-Ft. Worth, etc.— you may do readings more often if they are in different parts of the area.) Each time you read, present work you've never read publicly in that city before.

Giving a Reading

1. Practice reading your work aloud, so that you are comfortable, fluent, and easy to hear and follow.
2. Pick your material carefully. It should lend itself well to being read aloud, and it should be appropriate for your audience.
3. Plan to read for forty to sixty minutes if you are doing a solo reading, twenty to thirty-five minutes if you are on a double bill, even less if you are one of several readers. Time your material as you rehearse to make sure it runs the proper length of time.
4. If you will be reading at a bookstore (or any other organization that sells books), give the manager a list of all your published titles (including publishers and ISBN numbers) eight to ten weeks before your reading, so that copies of your books will be available. If you will be reading at an organization that doesn't sell books, bring copies with you to sign and sell on your own at the conclusion of the reading.
5. Don't expect huge crowds. An audience of twenty to twenty-five people is typical.

Arranging Book Signings

General Information

1. You may hold a book signing whenever you like. However, arrange most of your book signings for the following times:
   a. Within two months following the publication of your newest book. You may sign your earlier books at the same time as well.
   b. Immediately following a reading or lecture (usually, but not necessarily, at the same location).
   Book signings are occasionally held in conjunction with publication parties.
2. You may hold your signing at either a bookstore or a literary center. Avoid chain bookstores and used bookstores, however; both sponsor very few book signings. Signings at other locations are extremely rare.
3. Don't expect to sell lots of copies at a book signing. Selling fifteen to fifty copies is typical. Remember that the primary

purposes of a signing are to promote your work and attract attention to it, not to sell scads of copies.

4. Although many of the books you will sign will have been purchased on the spot, some people will bring in copies of books they already own for your signature. This is fine.

5. If you like, about three months before your new book is to be published, ask your publisher's promotion department to set up some book signings for you. However, don't expect much cooperation; most publishers will say no, or agree to set up at most one or two. Don't argue with this; set up your own signing(s) instead (or in addition).

6. While you want to be visible, you don't want to be ubiquitous. Set up no more than three book signings in the same metropolitan area per year—if possible, at two or more different locations. You may do more than three signings under these circumstances, however:

    a. In very large metro areas—Chicago, Los Angeles, southeast Florida, etc.—you may do signings more often if you spread them out among different parts of the metropolitan area.

    b. If you publish more than three new books in one year, you may do a signing for each new book.

    c. College and university bookstores have their own separate clienteles. You may do signings at these bookstores over and above the normal limit.

7. Do not expect to be paid anything to do a book signing.

Organizing a Book Signing

1. Contact the owner or manager of a bookstore you like, or the program director of a writers' center. It is usually best to make this initial contact by phone. If you wish to coordinate the signing with the publication of your newest book, make this call three months prior to its publication date.

2. Introduce yourself. Briefly mention your previous books (if any), their genres, and their publishers. If your new book is about to be published, say so; give its title, genre, publication date, publisher (if you're publishing it yourself, say so), and a brief description of it. Ask this person if they might be interested in sponsoring a book signing.

3. If your contact expresses an interest, offer to meet with them

and to send them any of the following:

    a. A list of all of your books, including publishers, genres, publication dates, ISBN numbers, and brief descriptions

    b. Copies of any of your previous books

    c. An advance copy or galleys of your newest book

If you meet with the manager, owner, or program director in person, bring these items with you to your meeting.

4. If the owner, manager, or program director says no (and many will; in arranging book signings you are playing the percentages just as much as when you submit your work to editors), repeat this process elsewhere as necessary.

5. Once a bookstore or literary center says yes to a signing, confirm that it has a complete list of all your past and future titles, and that it will order copies of most or all of these titles in time for them to arrive by the date of the signing. Exception: if the literary center does not have an in-house bookstore (and some don't), discuss who will provide copies of books to sell and sign.

6. If you will be selling books yourself, order them immediately. (In practice, you may order books from your publisher for resale *even if your contract specifically states that you may not resell any copies you order*. Every publisher I have talked with has confirmed this.)

7. A day or two before the signing, check in with the person organizing the event. Find out which books, if any, have not arrived. Offer to sell the bookstore or center copies of any missing books at 60 percent of the cover price. Bring these books with you to the signing.

8. Dress as you please for the signing. Bring several pens.

9. Arrive ten minutes early so that you can get comfortably set up.

10. If you will be selling books yourself, do the following:

    a. Bring a cash box, cash drawer, or envelope for making change.

    b. Bring plenty of change, including bills up to $10. Expect many purchases to be made with $20 bills. Be prepared to change a $50 or $100 bill.

    c. Decide in advance whether you will accept checks. Make sure all checks get made out to your name.

    d. You may sell your books at the cover price or at any lower price you choose.

e. In practice, you do not need to charge sales tax.

11. Be gracious to readers and customers. As much as possible, honor their requests for specific messages to accompany your signature.

12. If someone tries to hold your attention too long, politely say, "I'm sorry, but I need to be available to the next person now."

13. Thank the organizer of the reading afterward.

14. If you will be giving a reading or lecture and would like to sign (and perhaps sell) books afterward, check with your contact person to see if this is possible and to make any necessary arrangements.

9
Dealing With Agents

✔

✔

✔

20 Misconceptions About Agents

1. Once an agent has agreed to represent a project, it is as good as sold.
2. Once you have an agent, you can sit back and wait. You no longer need to work at building your writing career because your agent will take care of everything.
3. Agents sell most of the projects they represent.
4. Agents always have your best interests at heart, and will put your needs and interests before their own.
5. An agent is more interested in helping writers than in making money.
6. An agent will stick by you for years, whether or not they sell any of your work; your talent and potential are what count, not the amount of money you earn for your agent.
7. Most agents will be patient with a project, and submit it over and over until it sells, or has received many rejections.
8. Agents give the same service and attention to writers earning $5,000-$10,000 a year as they do to their bestselling authors.
9. You must be a career writer to get an agent; agents do not represent one- or two-project authors.
10. Once an agent accepts you as a client, they will represent any project you send them.
11. You can't sell a book without an agent.
12. The largest commercial book publishers and most television and film producers are happy to look at unagented manuscripts.
13. Most large and medium-sized book publishers give unagented manuscripts as much consideration and attention as they do agented work.
14. Once your agent has looked over and made changes in a contract, you do not have to look it over yourself, because the agent has caught and dealt with every problem.
15. The larger (or smaller, or better-known) a literary agency is, the better a job it will do for you.
16. If your agent moves to another agency, you may automatically move with them.
17. You may not have different agents representing different projects.

18. An agent's duties include offering criticism and editing.
19. Your agent should (or can, or will) act as publicist, teacher, psychologist, confessor, confidant, coach, cheerleader, source of comfort, spiritual advisor, surrogate parent, or friend.
20. Most agents do a good, thorough job for their clients.

29 Qualities of a Good Agent

A good agent:

1. Knows the market inside and out—including both large and small publishers (and/or production companies).
2. Keeps up with changes and developments in the industry.
3. Knows hundreds of editors, publishers, producers, and other industry people; gets along well with most of them; and knows what kinds of material those people appreciate or want to see.
4. Is a good promoter, salesperson, and negotiator.
5. Has a good sense of what each of your projects is worth, how much to ask for it, and who is most likely to be interested in it.
6. Has extensive experience as an agent and has made many sales. Ideally, the agent has sold many projects in the same field or genre as your own.
7. Goes to bat for you against publishers or producers whenever necessary.
8. Gets your work out to editors and/or producers promptly, and follows up all submissions when necessary.
9. Sends your work to at least three editors or producers at once (in the case of book proposals, at least four at once); sends a rejected manuscript back out again promptly. (Exception: in TV and film, it is common to send work to only one producer at a time.)
10. Continues to try to sell your work even after it has received some rejections; does not give up until the piece has been rejected at least fifteen times.
11. Has a good eye and instinct for what people (editors, publishers, producers, audiences, and readers) want.

12. Responds to your work, questions, letters, and phone calls promptly.
13. Is honest, straightforward, and cordial with you at all times.
14. Is willing to work with you if your material needs a small amount of rewriting, and can give good suggestions for doing that rewriting.
15. Reads and negotiates contracts carefully, thoroughly, and shrewdly.
16. Works with you on a project-by-project basis; does not demand exclusive rights to all your work.
17. Lets you know which editors and/or producers have seen and are currently looking at your material.
18. Gets you money, royalty statements, and important information promptly; forwards any mail, inquiries, and offers promptly.
19. Lets you know promptly when they have stopped trying to sell a piece that has been repeatedly rejected, and immediately permits you to market that piece on your own.
20. Has read extensively; enjoys both popular and literary material, and knows the difference between the two.
21. Lives in or near the following city, or visits it frequently:
    a. In the United States: New York (for plays and books); Los Angeles (for television and film)
    b. In Canada: Toronto
22. Earns a commission only on sales in which they were involved; does not expect a percentage of every dollar you earn as a writer.
23. Earns a living almost entirely from commissions, and does not charge fees for reading or submitting manuscripts.
24. Charges reasonable commissions (see "11 Tips on Author-Agent Agreements" on pages 161-162 for details).
25. Does not require potential clients to sign a release before agreeing to read their work.
26. Uses a fair, reasonable author-agent agreement (see pages 161-162 for details).
27. Supports you in your efforts to write what you wish to write, rather than what is popular this month, or what a publisher or producer has most recently asked for.
28. Believes in you and your ability as a writer.
29. Encourages you to write your best.

For more complete information on getting and working with an agent, consult *Literary Agents* by Michael Larsen (Writer's Digest Books) or *The Indispensable Writer's Guide* by Scott Edelstein (HarperCollins).

How an Agent Can Help Your Career

A good agent can:

1. Get your work into the hands of the editors, publishers, and/ or producers who are most likely to be interested in what you have to offer, and who are able to pay the most money for it.
2. Weed out the editors, publishers, and producers who are the most difficult to work with, the slowest to pay, the slowest to put books into print, or the least financially stable.
3. Encourage editors to respond to your work quickly, and can elbow them when they don't.
4. Negotiate publishing and/or production agreements on your behalf, thereby getting you the most money and the best terms.
5. Keep you informed of any important developments at your publisher(s), or within the industry as a whole.
6. Put pressure on publishers and producers on your behalf when they fail to pay on time, issue late or incomplete royalty statements, or fail to live up to any other items they have agreed to.
7. Promote you and your work to editors, publishers, and producers. This can result in unexpected opportunities such as a contract to write a book to a publisher's specs or a ghostwriting deal.
8. Serve as your representative to and liaison with the publishing (or film, television, etc.) industry.
9. Receive money and offers on your behalf, then bring them to you.
10. Offer professional advice.
11. Put you in touch with other people who can be helpful.

In contrast, a lazy, overworked, or underskilled agent can seriously harm your career by sending your work to the wrong people, reading and negotiating contracts haphazardly, or, worst of all, letting your work languish, unsubmitted, on their own desk.

Material Agents Do and Don't Represent

Many Agents Represent:
1. Novels and general-interest nonfiction for adults
2. Novels and general-interest nonfiction for young adults
3. Business books
4. Scripts for stage (all lengths)
5. Scripts, treatments, and concepts for film
6. Scripts, treatments, and concepts for television

A Few Agents Represent:
1. Video scripts
2. Computer software
3. Comics for syndication
4. Columns for syndication
5. Books for children, including picture books
6. Textbooks
7. Professional, medical, and technical books
8. Reference books
9. Literary novels

Agents Do Not Normally Represent:
1. Short story collections (except by authors whose novels they also represent)
2. Poetry collections (except in extraordinary cases)
3. Scholarly books
4. Nonfiction books for an extremely specialized and limited audience (e.g., *Teaneck, New Jersey: A History and Introduction*)
5. Short stories (except by superstar writers)
6. Poems
7. Essays and articles (except by superstar writers, or in book-length collections)
8. Greeting cards
9. Cartoons or cartoon ideas
10. Jokes for comedians
11. Radio or audio scripts
12. AV, audio, or video scripts for business and industry

13. Calendars
14. Advertising copy

Best Sources of Agents' Names and Addresses

General Lists of Agents

1. *Literary Market Place.* Reference book; published annually. Includes a comprehensive list of agents, but gives a limited amount of information on each.
2. *Guide to Literary Agents.* Reference book; published annually. Includes fewer agents, but each agent's interests, specialties, and credentials are described in excellent detail.
3. Member List, Association of Authors' Representatives, 10 Astor Place, 3rd floor, New York, NY 10003. A list of AAR members and an AAR brochure are available upon request; send a check or money order for $7 and a business-sized SASE with postage (or an SAE with one International Reply Coupon). This list includes names and addresses, and notes whether each agent handles print material; material for film, TV, and/or stage; or both.

Specialized Lists of Agents

1. *Children's Writer's and Illustrator's Market.* Reference book; published annually. Contains a list of many (though by no means all) of the agents who handle material for children and young adults. Each listing is very thorough.
2. *Dramatists Sourcebook.* Reference book; published annually.

Lists of Foreign Agents

1. *Directory of Publishing.* Reference book; published annually.
2. *International Literary Market Place.* Reference book; published annually.

4 Ways to Locate the Right Agent(s) for Your Work

1. Use the reference sources listed and described in "Best Sources of Agents' Names and Addresses" on page 156 and above.
2. Ask other people for information on any agents they have worked with or know something about. Folks you might talk to include:
   a. Writers you know
   b. Members of any professional writers' organization to which you belong
   c. Editors with whom you have built a respectful professional relationship (even if you've never sold them anything)
   d. Officers and staff of writers' organizations and/or writers' centers
   e. College teachers of creative and professional writing. Many of these people have agents, or knowledge of and experience with agents; nearly all keep regular office hours, and most are happy to talk on the phone or in person for a few minutes.
   f. Bookstore managers
   Ask about agents' effectiveness, responsiveness, willingness to stick with a project, knowledge of the market, strengths, weaknesses, etc.
3. Make a list of some North American writers who work in the same genre or area as your own project(s). (Exclude superstars.) Start with authors you admire. Scan the shelves at large libraries, bookstores, and newsstands to get other names. Then look up these writers in one or more of the following reference works, which are found at many large libraries:
   a. *Contemporary Authors*
   b. *Directory of American Poets and Fiction Writers*
   c. *International Authors and Writers Who's Who*
   d. *Something About the Author* (covers writers of children's and young adult material)
   e. *Who's Who in Writers, Editors, and Poets: U.S. and Canada*
   f. *Writers Directory*

The names (and sometimes addresses) of most writers' agents will be noted. Check the current address of any agent in one or more of the sources listed on pages 156-157.

4. You can also find out the names of authors' agents by calling those writers' publishers. Use *Books in Print* or *Forthcoming Books* to locate the initial North American publisher of one or more of an author's books. Call either the editorial department or the subsidiary rights department (sometimes called the rights and permissions department) of that publisher. Tell whomever answers, "I'm trying to find out the name of _____'s agent. Can you help me, or give me someone who can?"

19 Guidelines for Approaching Agents

1. Make a list of agents that seem appropriate for you and your work, using the guidelines on pages 157 and above.
2. Do not send unsolicited manuscripts to agents; get in touch and describe your project first.
3. Make your inquiry by mail unless you have a manuscript that is *extremely* timely. You may write to as many agents at a time as you like—eight to ten is typical. (Type each letter separately; form letters look amateurish.)
4. Write to specific agents by name; do not simply write to agencies.
5. Initial letters to agents resemble cover letters in some ways; follow tips 1-4, 6, 15-16, and 18-19 of "Writing a Cover Letter," on pages 111-113.
6. Your letter should be no longer than two pages; one to one-and-a-half pages is ideal.
7. In your first paragraph, introduce yourself, your writing career, and your experience *in one or two sentences*. For example, "I'm a novelist who has been writing since 1986, and who has published novels with Zebra Books and Leisure Books." If you have no significant publications and not much of a writing career so far, skip this paragraph.
8. Use your next two to six paragraphs to describe your project in detail. If it is nonfiction, explain its theme, audience, approach, purpose, and overall content in five paragraphs or less; also state whether it is in finished or proposal form. If it is fiction, or material for film, TV, or stage, write a very

brief plot synopsis (six paragraphs maximum). Indicate whether it is a finished, full-length work or a proposal, treatment, or one act. Begin your project description with a phrase such as, "I've just finished a novel entitled _____, which . . ."

9. In the paragraph that follows, discuss your publications and other credentials in more detail. Include any previous sales and publications likely to impress the editor, any significant writing awards or fellowships you've received, and any special experience you've had that informs your piece.

10. In your penultimate paragraph, ask if the agent would care to take a look at the project. (For example, "If this project intrigues you, please get in touch; I'd be happy to send it your way.")

11. If you prefer, you may outline or synopsize your project in a separate document runnning two to seven pages, either 1½- or double-spaced. Omit any outline or synopsis from your letter; instead, indicate that an outline is attached. (If you wish to have your outline returned, enclose a self-addressed envelope and sufficient return postage.)

12. If you like, you may discuss two (but no more than two) different projects in your inquiry letter. Your letter should still be no longer than two pages; if you're including separate synopses, these should run no longer than four pages each.

13. Enclose a #10 SASE for the agent's reply. If you've enclosed a separate outline and want it returned, provide sufficient return postage.

14. Expect responses in one to six weeks. Some agents prefer to write; others usually use the phone. Be wary of agents who take longer than six weeks unless they have been ill or on vacation.

15. Be very suspicious of any of the following:
    a. Agents who charge a fee to make submissions. Ignore them completely; they are not legitimate agents.
    b. Agents who charge a fee to read and consider your work. Either write back, politely but firmly offering to show them your work without paying a fee, or forget about them entirely.
    c. Agents who require you to sign a written release before

they will read your work. This is entirely unprofessional. Do not deal with these agents.

16. If an agent does not respond to your letter, forget about them. You may assume you are being deliberately ignored.

17. You may send your manuscript to as many agents at a time as you wish, unless one requests an exclusive look (sometimes called simply "an exclusive")—in which case do not send your project to that agent until such time as no other agent is reviewing it. When you send your work, include a self-addressed return envelope or mailing bag, return postage and a brief letter thanking the agent for his interest and reminding him of his request to see your manuscript.

18. If a publisher or producer offers to buy a book or script that you have submitted on your own, and you realize you need an agent to help work out a deal, do not contact agents by mail. Use the phone instead; as soon as you have given your name, explain that you have an offer that you need help negotiating.

19. You may approach agents outside North America just as you would agents in the United States and Canada. However, indicate who represents you here, if anyone. If your project has been published or produced in North America, state when and by whom. Write your letter of inquiry in English unless you are fluent in the appropriate language.

11 Tips on Author-Agent Agreements

1. Your agreement with your agent may be either written or oral, but both of you must clearly understand the terms. About half of all agents use written contracts, and half make simple oral agreements.

2. Author-agent agreements are almost always negotiable. Ask for and negotiate any changes that you need to; if the agent will not agree to terms you believe are reasonable, look for another agent.

3. *Do not assume that the terms you are offered are fair or standard.* Author-agent contracts vary widely. *Read any contract very carefully.* Agents (even some of the most effective ones) often protect their interests far more than yours in these agreements.

4. If an agent wants to make an oral agreement, ask for specific terms; if the agent says, "Standard terms" or "Standard commission," ask for details. (If the stated terms are limited to the size of their commission, this is ideal: it means that you and your agent can part ways whenever either of you chooses; that you are not obligated to let the agent handle your next work; and that they are not entitled to any money beyond any commissions.)

5. Do not agree to commissions higher than these:
   a. Material for television and film: 10 percent
   b. Books and other material for print publication: 15 percent; 25 percent for foreign sales; 25 percent for the sale of TV or film rights (15/20/20 percent is the norm)
   c. Plays: 15 percent; 20 percent for sales to stock and amateur companies; 25 percent for foreign sales; 25 percent for the sale of TV or film rights. (Many dramatic agents have lower commissions; 10/15/20/20 percent is not uncommon.)

6. Try to work on a project-by-project basis. Avoid giving an agent the right to represent your entire literary output. This gives the agent the right to do anything with each of your manuscripts, including nothing at all; at the same time, it forbids you from trying to sell anything on your own!

7. Ideally, your agreement should run until either of you wishes to end it (you may be required to give thirty or sixty

days' notice, which is fine). Do not let an agent represent your work for a specified period of time (usually one to three years). If an agent you want to work with absolutely insists on a fixed length of time, agree to a maximum of six months or one year.

8. Do not agree to give the agent a commission on every dollar you make from your writing, whether or not they were involved in the sale. A good agent should only want or expect a commission on sales that they made.

9. Do not agree to pay fees of any kind. However, if the agent wants to be reimbursed for reasonable incidental *expenses* (photocopying of manuscripts, overseas airmail postage, long-distance phone charges, etc.) related to selling your work, this is fine.

10. Try to get rid of any provision that requires you to let the agent represent your next project. If the agent insists on this provision and you're otherwise happy with the agreement, try to restrict it as much as possible; change "next project" to "next romance novel," "next nonfiction book for adults," etc.

11. If you make a written agreement, make sure it specifies that the agent will pay you your share of any money they receive within thirty days (in the case of checks drawn on foreign banks, within thirty days after the check clears). The agent should also agree to forward copies of royalty statements within thirty days.

26 Guidelines for Working With an Agent

1. Don't expect your agent to do all your career-building for you. Continue making and using professional contacts, gathering information, seeking endorsements for your work, etc.

2. Be polite, straightforward, honest, and businesslike at all times.

3. Write or call your agent whenever you need to, but otherwise be patient and keep mum. With few exceptions, agents have neither the time nor the inclination for a friendly chat.

4. Your agent will write or call whenever there is news to report. If you have heard little or nothing from your agent,

however, it is reasonable to call or write every four to six months to see what has happened.

5. Do not call your agent collect.

6. Once you have agreed to let an agent represent a project, provide them with the following information:
   a. The names, employing organizations, and addresses of any editors, producers, or directors who have asked to see your work.
   b. The names, employing organizations, and addresses of any editors, producers, or directors who have read and enjoyed your earlier work.
   c. The names of any editors, publishers, producers, directors or producing organizations that you do *not* want your work submitted to (if any).
   d. The names and employing organizations of any editors, producers, or directors who have already seen and rejected your project in its current (or very similar) form.
   e. Where, when, and by whom part or all of the project has been previously published or produced, if anywhere.

7. Be clear and explicit about what you want and need, especially when it comes to publishing and production contracts.

8. If there is a minimum amount of money that you must get for your project, or a specific amount you want your agent to ask for, let them know as soon as they have agreed to represent the manuscript.

9. Don't expect your agent to make decisions for you. Agents will bring you offers, answer your questions, and make suggestions, but only you can decide what to accept, what to turn down, when to ask for more, and how much more to ask for. Indeed, this is part of your responsibility as an agented author.

10. Let your agent know whether or not you would like to receive copies of rejection letters.

11. If your agent does not automatically send you a list of the people and organizations to which your project has been submitted, feel free to ask for it. Also feel free to ask for updates two or three times a year.

12. Allow your agent a reasonable amount of time to sell your work. Don't doubt the agent's effectiveness until a manuscript has received at least fifteen rejections. (If your

agent gives up on a piece before it has received at least a dozen rejections, it hasn't been given a decent chance.)

13. If you are having trouble of any kind with a publisher or producing organization, let your agent know, especially if it involves money. It is your agent's job to try to straighten things out for you.

14. If you ever have a problem with your *agent*, write, or (preferably) call them to discuss the issue. Be honest, firm, forthright, calm, and concerned.

15. Remember that your agent has many other clients. Expect them to be responsive and helpful—but don't expect constant and immediate availability.

16. Don't let publishers or producers make an end run around your agent. If you are approached directly about a project your agent is representing, don't agree to any terms. Don't even indicate what terms or how much money you want. Instead, get the person's name, phone number, and employer, and pass on this information to your agent, who will take things from there. This is not only good business, it's your legal obligation. (You *may* answer questions from a publisher or producer that are not about money or rights— e.g., "When do you think you can have the project finished?")

17. If your agent is approached about a project of yours which they are not representing, they will refer the inquiry to you. They will not ask for, nor are they entitled to, a fee or commission for this referral.

18. It is not necessary to ask whether your agent would be interested in seeing further projects. Simply send each new project to your agent with a short cover letter. (But don't inundate the agent with your work—it's rude and unprofessional. Furthermore, most agents will handle no more than two or three projects by the same writer at once.)

19. When you send your agent a new project, expect a response in two to eight weeks. If necessary, make a polite but firm follow-up call after two months. After three months, unless the agent has been ill or on a long vacation, you have a problem: the agent isn't doing their job.

20. Your agent has the right to decline to represent any future project you send.

21. If you want to discuss an idea for a new project, have a

business-related question, or need some professional advice, feel free to call or write your agent. Be reasonable, though: limit phone calls to ten to twenty minutes, and don't badger your agent with constant questions and ideas.

22. Don't expect your agent to get excited about your work; from their point of view, it's just a commodity to be sold. If your agent does get excited, don't be surprised if the excitement disappears after the project is sold—or after it has been rejected a few times.

23. When an agent says, "I'm sure I can sell this project," never assume that they will—or that they won't. No one ever really knows what publishers and producers will buy—including the publishers and producers themselves.

24. If your agent asks to be reimbursed for reasonable expenses such as photocopying and overseas airmail costs, do so within three weeks. Do not ask to have these charges deducted from your future earnings.

25. If you expect to be out of town for more than two or three days, let your agent know when, where, and how to reach you.

26. If your agent drops you as a client after failing to sell one or more of your projects, don't be surprised or angry. Agents constantly take on new clients, then drop all but the most successful ones later.

How to Fire Your Agent Gracefully

If you are having a problem with your agent, it is usually best to discuss the problem honestly. If this does not work, or if the agent simply isn't selling your work or is doing a poor job, follow these guidelines:

1. If you have a written agreement with your agent, read it over carefully. Follow its provisions for ending your relationship to the letter. If you have no written agreement, skip to the next step.

2. Write a brief, polite, firm, businesslike letter to your agent. In it state the following:
   a. You no longer think that your relationship is beneficial to you.

b. You wish to cease to be the agent's (and, if appropriate, the agency's) client.
c. The agent shall make no more submissions of any of your work.
d. The agent shall remain your representative on any submissions that are still live, for a period of sixty days.
e. You wish to receive a list of all organizations (publishers and/or production companies) and people (editors, producers, and/or directors) who have rejected any of your unsold works. Also ask for a list of people and organizations that are still considering your material. Ask the agent to inform you of any offers and/or rejections that result from these submissions.
f. The agent shall continue to receive royalty statements and money on your behalf for deals they have already made for you; they shall forward all statements and your share of any money to you within thirty days of their receipt of such statements and money.
g. (Optional) All of your manuscripts still in the agent's possession or rejected in the future shall be returned to you.
h. This shall take effect immediately (or on some specific date noted in your author-agent agreement).

You do not need to explain or justify your reason for ending your relationship. Mail the letter; keep a copy for your files.

3. *Do not feel guilty*. At worst, the agent will regret losing some potential revenue; you certainly won't leave emotional scars. Clients leave agents, and agents dump clients, all the time. Almost always, it is because neither of them is making any (or enough) money.

4. Look for a new, better agent—or start sending your work out on your own.

10
Keeping Track of Business

☑

☑

☑

Keeping a Calendar or Datebook

A calendar is useful for any businessperson; it is especially helpful for writers. Here are some important items to note in your datebook:

1. Upcoming meetings (including what to bring, what to wear, what topics to discuss, etc.).
2. Deadlines for assignments, other writing projects, the return of galleys, etc.
3. Dates by which you expect responses from editors, producers, and agents (see "11 Things to Do When an Editor is Slow to Respond" on pages 116-117 for details). If you have heard no word by this date, make a follow-up call.
4. Dates on which royalty statements are due.
5. Dates by which you expect to be paid by clients, publishers, or agents; payments not made by these dates are past due and should be followed up.
6. Future publication or performance dates for your work.
7. Deadlines for paying your federal and state estimated tax.

Keeping a Submission Book

A submission book is an excellent way to keep track of who is considering each of your manuscripts.

1. Use whatever style of book works best for you: a spiral notebook, a loose-leaf binder, a bound blank book, or even loose sheets in a file folder.
2. For convenience and simplicity, use a separate page for each manuscript, and follow the same format on each page.
3. Arrange your pages alphabetically, if possible, according to manuscript titles. Loose-leaf binders and loose sheets in folders are ideal for this; if you are using a bound book, leave a few blank pages between entries. These can be filled in later, as you write new material.
4. At the top of each page, write the title of the manuscript.
5. Divide the page into five columns. The first four should each be about an inch wide (on $8\frac{1}{2}" \times 11"$ or $8" \times 10"$ paper); the

fifth should take up the right half of the page. Title these columns as follows: Publication (or Publisher, or Producing Organization); Editor (or Producer, or Director); Date Sent; Date Reply Received; Comments.

6. Whenever you send out a manuscript, fill in the first three columns; when you receive a reply, fill in the last two. Under "Comments" you might simply write, "Rejected," "Sold for $600," "Rewrite requested; mailed 8/19," etc. Or, if you prefer, you might write in (or synopsize) each editor's comments. Use this column however you wish.

7. Look through your submission book at least twice a month, and note which submissions require following up.

8. If an editor or producer is slow to respond to a manuscript, note your follow-up in the "Comments" column—e.g., "Follow-up phone call, 4/2; call returned 4/3, asked for two more weeks to consider."

9. A submission book can also be used to track queries, letters requesting assignments, delivery of assignments, letters of inquiry to agents, consideration of your work by agents, submission of your work by agents, etc.

Setting Up a Filing System

Only you can determine exactly what filing system will work best for you. However, the following tips should prove helpful:

1. The guiding principles for any good filing system are simplicity, ease of access, and ease of use.

2. Keep all your files in alphabetical order in one place—ideally, in a filing cabinet. Keep your submission book and your calendar or datebook nearby. If you like, keep your journal nearby as well.

3. Make a separate file for each of your pieces. Begin a new file as soon as you begin work on a piece, even if all you have so far are scraps or notes.

4. Title each file with the title of your piece. If you don't have a final (or any) title yet, come up with a tentative, working title. As necessary, change the title of both the piece and the file.

5. Keep everything pertaining to a piece in its file. As much as

possible, establish a standard order for items within all your files; this makes things easier to find. For example, you might place research materials first; notes next; then drafts 1, 2, 3, etc.; final draft; cover letter or assignment query; contract for initial publication; contracts for reprint uses; correspondence related to the piece; and miscellaneous items.

6. Keep a copy of all relevant documents and information indefinitely. It's better to keep something too long than to discard it prematurely.

7. Keep a separate file on every current and previous client. You may either keep these separate or integrate them alphabetically with your other files.

8. Make and keep files for other relevant items, e.g., miscellaneous notes and ideas, your will, tax records for the year, etc.

Keeping Tax Records

1. It is not necessary to keep formal accounts as a bookkeeper would, nor do you need a ledger book. However, it is necessary to keep complete and accurate lists of all income and expenses.

2. Keep a separate, dated list of all expenses for each general category of expenditures — e.g., postage, photocopying and printing, office supplies, long-distance calls, books and magazines, business meals, travel expenses, educational expenses, etc.

3. Make up a page for miscellaneous and unusual expenses. Keep a dated list of all such expenses.

4. Keep a dated list of all payments you receive. Include the name of the person or organization that paid each sum.

5. Keep copies of receipts for all business expenses. When a receipt contains both business and personal items, circle the business items. When a single item is for both personal and business use, circle it and write down the amount that is business-oriented. It is not necessary to order these receipts; you won't need them unless you're audited. Place them randomly in a file or box.

6. On a separate page, determine and note the monthly cost of maintaining your workspace, if appropriate. Include the

appropriate portion of your rent or mortgage payment, utility costs, repairs, etc.

7. On another separate page, keep a dated record of any business-related miles you drive.

8. Hang onto your tax records (including receipts) indefinitely—at the very least for seven years. The tax people have been known to question people's income and expenses several years after the fact.

Preparing Your Federal Income Tax Return

The following tips will help you to save money and time when filling out and filing your U.S. federal income taxes:

General Information

1. You will need, at minimum, the following forms and schedules:
   a. Form 1040 (*not* 1040-A or 1040-EZ)
   b. Schedule C
   c. Schedule SE
   d. State tax forms

   You may also need:
   e. City or county tax forms
   f. Form 4562 (Depreciation)
   g. W-2s from employers
   h. Copies of any 1099-MISC forms you've received
   i. Copies of any 1040-ES forms you've filed (or the information therefrom)
   j. Any other forms relevant to your personal situation (e.g., Schedule A, Schedule E1C)
   k. Form 8829 (Expenses for Business Use of Your Home)

   Items a, b, c, and f appear in the standard 1040 booklet. You will also need to gather together all your income and expense records for the year.

2. Order and refer to the following IRS publications, if you do not have them already:
   a. The 1040 information/forms booklet (includes Schedules A, B, C, C-EZ, D and SE, Forms 1040 and 4562, and other items)
   b. IRS Publication 17: *Your Federal Income Tax*
   c. Publication 334: *Tax Guide for Small Businesses*

d. Publication 535: *Business Expenses*

e. Publication 553: *Highlights of Tax Changes*

f. Publication 587: *Business Use of Your Home*

g. Publication 917: *Business Use of a Car*

All IRS publications and forms are available free of charge by calling 800-829-3676 or visiting an IRS office. Many are also available free at banks, post offices, and libraries. All IRS forms and publications change annually.

3. Obtain multiple copies of each blank form; photocopy extra copies if necessary (most libraries have masters of all forms and schedules). This gives you the freedom to make mistakes and corrections. Use pencil, for the same reason.

4. Fill out your tax forms in the following order:

   a. Schedule C

   b. Schedule SE

   c. Form 1040

   d. State tax forms

   e. Local tax forms

   If you need to use Form 4562 and/or Form 8829 (many writers do), fill out these before anything else; if you choose to itemize personal as well as business deductions, fill out Schedule A before preparing Form 1040.

5. Be honest. Claim every deduction you deserve and declare every penny you earn from your writing; do not claim any spurious, inflated, or imaginary deductions.

6. You may round off figures to the nearest dollar; round 50¢ or more up, 49¢ or less down.

7. You may use a loss on your Schedule C to reduce your overall income, thus reducing your income taxes; however, normally you may not declare a loss on Schedule C for more than two consecutive years, or more than two years out of any five. (Note: a loss on Schedule C will not entitle you to a refund of any Social Security tax withheld *from your salary* during the year.)

8. If you have incurred an expense for both business and personal purposes, you may deduct only the business part; in the case of travel, deduct the amount the trip would have cost you if it had been for business only.

9. Triple-check all your entries and math before sending in any forms.

10. If you have questions, consult one or more of the following:
    a. A professional tax preparer.
    b. The IRS's information staff; call the local number or
       800-829-1040. (Avoid asking complex or difficult
       questions of these people—they can't answer them.)
    c. Tele-Tax: recorded information on a wide range of tax
       topics. Check with the IRS or in your phone book for
       the number in your area.
    d. One or more of the publications listed in item 2 above.
    e. A tax preparation guide, such as the one recommended
       in item 13 below.
11. For your own protection, make and keep copies of
    everything you send to the IRS.
12. Unless you expect the federal tax on your income to be
    under $500 for the entire year, the IRS expects you to make
    quarterly estimated tax payments by April 15, June 15,
    September 15, and January 15. Most states expect you to
    do the same with your state taxes.
13. For more detailed information on taxes for writers, see "A
    Writer's Guide to Income Taxes" by Scott Edelstein, in *A
    Beginner's Guide to Getting Published*, edited by Kirk
    Polking (Writer's Digest Books). An excellent general guide
    to federal income taxes is the annual *Guide to Income Tax
    Preparation* by Warren H. Esanu, Barry Dickman, Elias M.
    Zuckerman, and Michael N. Pollet (Consumer Reports
    Books).

Preparing Schedule C

1. If you operate two or more different types of businesses
   (e.g., freelance writing and auto repair), you must fill out a
   separate Schedule C for each area of business activity.
2. List 6676 as your principal business code at the top of the
   page. Leave the box marked "Employer ID number" blank.
3. Under "Principal business or profession," write "writing,"
   "writing and editing," "literary services," etc.
4. If you don't have a name for your business (most writers
   do not), write "No name" under "Business name and
   address"; if you use a pen name, list it as your business
   name. If you have no separate business address, fill in your
   home address.

5. Under "Method(s) used to value closing inventory," check "Does not apply."
6. Under "Accounting method," check "Cash."
7. Answer "yes" to the question, "Did you 'materially participate' in the operation of this business?"
8. List the total of all your writing/editing income in Part I. Except in highly unusual circumstances, write "0" on the lines marked "Returns and allowances," "Cost of goods sold," and "Other income."
9. List all your writing expenses in Part II. Deductible expenses include:
   a. Postage and shipping
   b. Printing, photocopying, and other duplicating
   c. Office supplies
   d. Office equipment and furniture (including computers, fax machines, desks, etc.). Several complex provisions apply; see Publication 534, *Depreciation*, and Publication 535, *Business Expenses*, for details. You may need to use Form 4562.
   e. Professional services (attorneys, manuscript typists, etc.)
   f. Travel (including hotel, cabs, tolls, tips, etc.)
   g. Business-related meals and entertainment (including drinks and tips); your deduction is limited to 80 percent of the actual cost
   h. Long-distance phone calls and faxes (including applicable taxes)
   i. Advertising
   j. Professional dues
   k. Books, magazines, and other publications
   l. Business use of your car—either the actual cost or a flat rate per mile traveled, plus parking, tolls, etc. If you take this deduction, you must fill out a small part of Form 4562, Depreciation.
   m. Any other expense directly related to your writing (e.g., the cost of renting a VCR and several movies for an article on Woody Allen's films)
   n. Sales tax on all of the above items
   o. Educational expenses (including tuition, books, supplies, etc.) if that education augments your ability in an area *in which you are already a trained, working professional.*

p. The cost of your workspace, including utilities and repairs, *if the workspace (whether a separate structure, a room in your home, or a part of a room) is used exclusively (or almost exclusively) for your work.* Several complex provisions apply; see Publication 587, *Business Use of Your Home*, for details. You must file 8829.

q. Any other legitimate expense related to your writing. List the total of all expenses in each category. Most of these categories are not listed on Schedule C; you will have to add them. Attach an additional page if necessary, and write "See attached page" at the end of Part II.

10. You may *not* deduct any of the following costs:
    a. Local telephone service (unless you have a second line that is used at least partly for business)
    b. Expenses involved in commuting to a job
    c. Workspace expenses, if you use your workspace for personal as well as business purposes
    d. Educational expenses, if the education does not augment your skill in an area in which you are already a trained, working professional

11. You may deduct 30 percent of the amount you paid for health insurance or HMO coverage during the year *on your 1040 form*, not on Schedule C.

12. If your total income from writing, editing and related endeavors totaled $25,000 or less for the year; *and* you had business expenses totaling $2,000 or less; *and* you are not declaring a loss; *and* you are not filing Forms 4562 (Depreciation) or 8829 (Expenses for Business Use of Your Home), then you may normally file Schedule C-EZ instead of Schedule C. Schedule C-EZ is very brief and simple to fill out, and requires no itemization of expenses.

11
Legal Matters

☞

☞

☞

11 Key Points of an Assignment Agreement

Whether written or oral, the agreement you make with a publisher concerning a piece to be written on assignment should normally contain the following provisions:

1. Specifications for your piece:
   a. Its working title
   b. The agreed-upon length (normally in words or pages)
   c. A very brief description of the piece (e.g., "an overview for the general reader of recent technological developments in robotics")
2. The date by which the completed piece must be received by the publisher. (Set a reasonable deadline; try to build in a little extra time for your protection.)
3. The amount of your payment and the date by which it will be due. (Avoid payment on publication; as much as possible, tie all deadlines for payment to your delivery date.)
4. Provisions for dealing with an unacceptable manuscript:
   a. The editor's obligation to inform you within a reasonable time (usually one month, never more than two) that the piece is unacceptable.
   b. The editor's obligation to give you specific suggestions and parameters for rewriting the piece, and to set a reasonable amount of time to do the rewrite (usually at least sixty days, often more).
   c. Your right to refuse to do a rewrite, accept a kill fee instead, and retain all rights to your piece.
   d. The editor's right to find the rewrite unacceptable, pay you a kill fee, and return all rights to the piece to you.
5. The amount of your kill fee, should one be necessary. This should be no less than 25 percent of the agreed-upon price of the piece, and ideally 30-40 percent. (In book publishing, the terms are somewhat different; see "25 Key Points of a Book Contract" on pages 179-186 for details.)
6. The specific rights the publisher is buying. (See "Determining Which Rights to Sell" on pages 196-199 for more details.)
7. Provisions covering any special arrangements (e.g.,

illustrations, photographs, a press pass, or payment of your expenses by the publisher).
8. The number of author's copies you will receive on publication (five is standard for magazines, twenty-five for books).
9. Signatures of both parties; initials of both parties to accompany any changes; a date accompanying your signature.
10. Your agreement should be in writing, except in the following cases:
    a. If it is with a newspaper or newsletter; these usually rely on oral contracts. If you *are* offered a written agreement, however, do not refuse it.
    b. If it is with a very small magazine *and* your fee will be $50 or less.
    c. In circumstances where you expect to make no or next-to-no money.
11. Items 3, 4, and 5 above are not necessary in cases where no money will change hands.

8 Key Points of a Magazine, Newspaper, Newsletter or Anthology Contract

1. Basic information:
   a. The names and addresses of both parties
   b. The title of the piece
   c. The date of the agreement
2. The rights being purchased. (See "Determining Which Rights to Sell" on pages 196-199 for details.)
3. How much and when you are to be paid. Avoid payment on publication, which can delay money indefinitely (or keep you from being paid at all if the publisher fails to publish your piece); try to be paid in full on acceptance. If this is impossible, try to be paid half on acceptance, half three months (six months maximum) later.
4. Editing provisions. Possible options:
   a. All editing shall be subject to your approval. (This is ideal, and means that you will be sent a copyedited manuscript and/or galleys for your examination and correction.)

b. The publication may edit your work as it sees fit, but shall do so with great care. (Variation: all editing shall be reasonable and appropriate.)

c. The publication may edit your work as it sees fit.

d. No editing provision. (In this event, item c is implied.)

If you are concerned about being badly edited, or if the publication has edited your work badly in the past, ask for (and if need be, insist on) item a. Otherwise, go along with b, c, or d until and unless you have reason not to.

5. Provisions for illustrations or photographs, if any.

6. Royalty provisions (for anthologies only). See tip 6 in "Determining Which Rights to Sell" on pages 196-199 for details.

7. Author's copies. The following terms are standard; ask for them if necessary:

a. Magazines and newsletters: five copies.

b. Paperback anthologies: two or three copies of the initial edition; one copy of each reprint edition.

c. Hardcover anthologies: one or two copies of the initial edition; one copy of each reprint edition.

Newspapers virtually never give out free copies officially, though if you stop by the editorial offices you can usually take home half a dozen at no charge.

8. Signatures of both parties; initials of both parties to accompany any changes; a date to accompany your signature; your social security number (if requested).

25 Key Points of a Book Contract

1. Basic information:

a. The names and addresses of both parties.

b. The tentative title of the book (and, in some cases, a brief description of it).

c. The required length of the completed manuscript (for a book sold on the basis of a proposal).

d. The date of the agreement.

2. Delivery date (if the manuscript is not yet finished). Be sure to set a deadline you can reasonably meet; for your protection, build in at least two months of extra time.

3. Advance (if any):
    a. The amount to be paid on signing.
    b. The amount to be paid on acceptance of the finished manuscript (if the book is not yet complete).
    c. Any amount to be paid on delivery of portions of the manuscript.
    d. Any amount to be paid after acceptance of the full manuscript.

    Most publishers pay the full advance on signing if the book is complete, half on signing and half on acceptance if the book still needs to be written (or needs rewriting). Push hard for these terms; if absolutely necessary, accept a small portion (no more than 25 percent) of the advance after delivery — three, six, or (at the very most) nine months thereafter. Avoid payment on publication, which can delay your money indefinitely, and keep you from being paid at all if the book is not published.

4. Royalties:
    a. When they are to be paid. The standard is semiannually; insist on this. Exception: allow very small publishers, especially very small scholarly presses, to issue statements once a year.
    b. Lag-time between the end of a royalty period and the issuing of a statement (and, when appropriate, a check) for that period. This should be no longer than three months. Two is not uncommon.
    c. Royalty rates (see "Standard Royalty Rates for Books" on pages 186-188 for details).
    d. Provisions for reduced royalties (see "Standard Royalty Rates for Books" on pages 186-188 for details).
    e. The maximum **reserve against returns**: the percentage of the royalty income during any period that may be held over until the following statement by the publisher as an insurance policy against the possibility of unsold copies being returned for credit. Insist on a specific percentage (*not* "a reasonable reserve") — no more than 50 percent for mass-market paperbacks, 30 percent for all other types of books.
    f. What information each royalty statement must provide. Press hard to make this description part of your contract: "Each statement shall list the number printed, sold, and

returned, and the appropriate royalty rates (and credits in dollars and cents), for all editions at all prices, as well as the current reserve for returns for all editions at all prices."

   g. When royalty statements will stop being issued. You should continue to receive statements for every royalty period in which copies are sold; the publisher should not be permitted to cease issuing statements and checks as soon as your book goes out of print.

5. Auditing:
   a. Your right to have an auditor examine the publisher's accounts at any reasonable time, with sufficient advance notice.
   b. The publisher's obligation to pay for the audit if it turns up errors in the publisher's favor of 5 percent or more, and to promptly pay you the amount in error.
   c. Your obligation to pay for the audit if the errors are in your favor or if they are in the publisher's favor by less than 5 percent; your publisher's obligation to correct the error on the next royalty statement and adjust the amount it owes you (or you owe it) accordingly.

6. Rights purchased/subsidiary rights:
   a. Which rights the publisher controls; which rights you control.
   b. How money received by the publisher from the sale of any subsidiary rights is to be shared (e.g., split equally, or 75 percent to you and 25 percent to the publisher, etc.).
   c. Your publisher's obligation to notify you of any subsidiary rights sale it makes, and to inform you of the details of the sale (amount of money, length and territory of the license, etc.), within sixty days.

7. Provision for competitive and simultaneous works. It is reasonable for your publisher to insist that you not publish another book that will *directly* compete with the one it is buying until that book goes out of print. Do *not*, however, stand for any of these provisions:
   a. You warrant that the book will be your next work.
   b. You warrant that you will not work on another project while writing the current book.
   c. You may not sell (or even write) another book until the

publisher accepts (or publishes) the current book.

    d. You may not publish another book on the same subject, even if it will not directly compete with the book you're selling.

8. The date by which the publisher must publish the book or lose the right to do so; the circumstances under which this time limit may be extended (war, natural disaster, acts of God, etc.). Eighteen months from acceptance is standard; agree to two years only if you absolutely must.

9. Indexing, illustrations, photographs, an introduction by another writer, etc.:

    a. Who will provide them.

    b. Who will pay for them.

    c. How you will pay for any items you are responsible for—out of the advance, out of your own pocket, or by other means. In the case of an index, ask your publisher to arrange for the indexing for you and to charge the cost against future earnings in your royalty account; this is far better than paying for the indexing by check.

10. Information on prior publication. If any portion of the book has already been sold or published, you must indicate in your contract which portion, and when and where it appeared. You must also provide copyright information on previous publication.

11. Right of refusal (for books sold on the basis of a proposal):

    a. The terms under which the publisher may choose not to accept the book for publication. Push hard for language that allows the publisher to say no only if the manuscript is incomplete or not fit for publication; avoid language that allows the publisher to refuse to accept a manuscript for any reason, or that allows its own judgment to be final and uncontestable.

    b. The publisher's obligation to supply specific guidance for rewriting if the finished manuscript is unfit for publication, and your time limit for doing such a rewrite. Make sure you get at least ninety days—more, if the book will be lengthy.

    c. What happens if the publisher deems your rewrite unacceptable, or if you refuse to do a rewrite in the manner it requests (or at all). Possible options to be specified in the contract: the matter goes to arbitration;

the contract is cancelled and all rights revert to you; the publisher may bring in an outside writer at its own expense — or, worse, at yours. Either of the first two options is fine; the third is clearly unacceptable.

    d. In the event that the contract is cancelled, what becomes of the advance money already paid. Possible options: you retain it; you must immediately return it; you must return it *only if* you sell the book to another publisher; you must return only a portion of it. Push for the first option, of course. Important: if the contract has been cancelled because the publisher does not find your book satisfactory, you are no longer entitled to any advance money not yet paid (except for any previous delinquent payments).

12. Galleys/page proofs/right to edit:
    a. The publisher's obligation to send you galleys and/or page proofs for your correction.
    b. Your obligation to correct and return galleys and/or page proofs within a reasonable time (usually ten business days).
    c. Your right to final authority over all editing.

13. Legal protection:
    a. Your guarantee that nothing in your book is libelous, illegal, or (to the best of your knowledge) false or inaccurate.
    b. What you and the publisher shall do in the event either or both of you are sued because of the book. Agree to jointly choose an attorney and split the cost of defending any lawsuit; do not allow the publisher to make you responsible for all of its lawyer's fees.
    c. The publisher's obligation to provide you with libel insurance to cover the book. (This provision is rare; you're fortunate if you get it.)

14. Author's alterations: if the changes you make in the galleys and/or page proofs (except those that correct typesetter's errors) result in costs that are more than or equal to 10 percent of the cost of initially typesetting your manuscript, you are obligated to pay the amount of these costs over 10 percent (*not* the full cost of making all corrections). Try to get this cost charged to your account instead of payable by check.

15. Manuscript preparation:
    a. How many copies you agree to deliver (normally one or two).
    b. Manuscript format (for example, double-spaced hard copy, or on disc, using a standard word processing program, etc.).
    c. Inclusion and delivery of illustrations, charts, graphs, permissions for reprinting previously published material, etc.
16. Under whose name the book will be copyrighted. This should be either your name or your pen name, as you prefer. Exception: textbooks are usually copyrighted in the name of the publisher.
17. Author's copies:
    a. The number of copies of the first edition you shall receive at no charge. Twenty-five is standard; push for it.
    b. The number of copies you shall receive of each subsequent edition (and each simultaneous edition in another format) published by the same publisher. Ten is normal.
    c. The publisher's promise to make its best efforts to secure for you free copies of editions published by other publishers, if those editions result from deals the publisher makes on your behalf.
    d. Your right to buy additional copies at a discount at any time. This discount should be at least 40 percent. Try to have the cost of additional author's copies charged to your royalty account instead of payable immediately by check. Your contract will prohibit you from reselling any copies you buy; in practice, however, you *may* resell them so long as you do not (except under highly unusual circumstances) sell them to bookstores or other retailers.
18. What happens if the publisher files for bankruptcy or reorganization. Try to get language that requires the publisher to either cancel your contract when it files, or, if it chooses to keep your contract in force, to immediately pay off all outstanding debts to you.
19. Option clause: your obligation to give the publisher the first look at your next book. Try to get rid of this completely; if

that is not possible, try to limit it in one or more of these ways:

a. Give the publisher an option only on your next book of the same type—your next mystery novel for young adults, your next adult nonfiction trade book, etc.

b. Give yourself the option of submitting either your next book *or* your next book proposal.

c. Give the publisher no more than sixty days to consider your next book or proposal; get rid of any language that allows it to withhold a decision on your next book until after your current book is completed or published.

d. Give yourself the right to turn down the publisher's offer on your next book if you find the offer unsatisfactory. The following language will work well: "The Publisher shall have the first option to publish the Author's next book, provided its terms for that book are fair and reasonable, and within industry norms."

20. Arrangements regarding revised and updated editions (for nonfiction books):

a. The publisher's right to publish revised or updated editions *by mutual arrangement*. Do not give the publisher the right to publish such an edition without your consent.

b. The publisher's obligation to pay you a new (usually smaller) advance to prepare a new edition. The amount of the advance may be specified, or it may be *mutually* decided upon later.

c. The publisher's right to treat revised and updated editions as new books for the purposes of computing royalties—for example, a revised edition of a hardcover trade book would earn a 10 percent royalty on the first 5,000 copies sold, no matter how many copies the earlier edition sold.

21. Out-of-print provisions:

a. How it shall be determined that your book is out of print. Insist that your book automatically be considered out of print if it is unavailable from the publisher for a period of ninety days or more. Do *not* settle for language that keeps your book in print until the publisher declares it out of print, or that keeps your contract in force if the publisher no longer makes it available for sale but the book is in print in one or more editions published by *other* presses.

   b. Your specific procedure for reclaiming any unexercised rights once your book has gone out of print.

   c. The publisher's right to put your book back into print within a strictly limited time (usually six months) once it has gone out of print. If it fails to do so, then all unexercised rights return to you.

22. Remainders/overstock: your right to purchase overstock (excess copies of your book sitting in your publisher's warehouse) and/or remainders (copies remaining in the warehouse when your book goes out of print) at the below-wholesale remainder/overstock price before those copies are offered to anyone else at that price.

23. A provision for referring any unresolvable conflicts to a mutually acceptable arbitrator, whose decision shall be legally binding on both parties. This very important clause enables you and your publisher to resolve disagreements without going to court. Push hard for this provision if it is not already part of your contract.

24. Agency clause (if an agent is involved): a provision requiring the publisher to send all money and royalty statements to your agent.

25. Signatures of both parties (and, usually, of witnesses); initials of both parties to accompany any changes; a date to accompany your signature (if requested); your social security number (if requested).

Standard Royalty Rates for Books

Royalties may be figured on the cover or retail price (the price printed on the book cover or jacket); the invoice price (the cover price less a small shipping allowance, usually 50-75¢ per copy); the wholesale price (the price charged to bookstores and book distributors); or the net receipts (the actual amount received by the publisher).

1. Hardcover trade books for adults: 10 percent of the cover or invoice price for the first 5,000 copies; 12½ percent on the next 5,000; 15 percent thereafter.
2. Hardcover trade books for children and young adults: rates range from a flat 10 percent of the cover or invoice price to the rates for adult trade hardcovers.
3. Trade paperbacks for adults: 6 to 8 percent of the cover or invoice price, sometimes more for sales above 50,000 copies.
4. Trade paperbacks for children and young adults: 5 to 7½ percent of the cover or invoice price.
5. Mass-market paperbacks for adults: 8 percent of the cover price, sometimes more for sales above 100,000 or 150,000 copies.
6. Mass-market paperbacks for children and young adults: 6 to 8 percent of the cover price.
7. Textbooks: 10 to 15 percent of net receipts for college texts; 6 to 15 percent of net receipts for elementary, junior high, and high school texts.
8. Professional, technical, medical, and reference books (except trade reference works): 10 to 15 percent of net receipts (for publishers that use a net receipts base); 10 to 15 percent of the cover or invoice price (for publishers that use these bases).
9. Scholarly books: 10 to 15 percent of net receipts (for publishers that use a net receipts base); 10 to 15 percent of the cover or invoice price (for publishers that use these bases).
10. Base your computations on the type of book you wish to sell, not the type of publisher you believe you are dealing with. Presses such as St. Martin's, Basil Blackwell, and the University of California Press publish both trade and scholarly books; St. Martin's publishes texts as well.
11. Exceptions to the above:
    a. Some trade publishers base their royalties on wholesale prices or net receipts instead of retail or invoice prices. This is fine so long as the percentages are proportionately higher, so that the resulting dollar amounts are roughly equal to those that would result from the standard royalty rates described in items 1 through 6 above.

b. Very small presses, especially literary presses, often pay royalty rates that are 10 to 50 percent lower than those noted in items 1 and 3 above.

c. Royalties on art books, children's picture books, other heavily illustrated books, and other books that are very expensive to manufacture are often 10 to 50 percent lower than those noted in items 1 through 4 above.

12. Most publishers pay reduced royalties on books sold under unusual circumstances. Here are some of these circumstances:

a. Books sold outside the United States and/or Canada.

b. Books sold at a discount of 50 percent or more, including books sold to wholesalers and distributors.

c. Books sold to or through book clubs.

d. Books sold through mail order.

e. Braille or large print editions intended for the visually impaired.

f. Books sold to organizations in bulk for distribution to their members, clients, customers, or employees.

g. Books sold through other unusual means.

13. Typical net receipts for various types of books are as follows:

a. Trade books: 50 to 60 percent of the retail or invoice price.

b. Textbooks: 80 percent of the retail or invoice price.

c. Professional, technical, medical, and reference (except trade reference) books: 65 to 80 percent of the retail or invoice price.

35 Important Things to Remember When Negotiating a Publishing Agreement

1. Try to enter into any negotiation with these principles in mind:

a. Both parties want to come to an agreement, and it is in their best interests to do so.

b. Both parties will work in good faith to come to an agreement.

c. Don't expect to get everything you ask for.

d. Each party wants to get the best deal it can.

    e. If a mutually acceptable agreement cannot be reached, you will be willing to scrub the whole deal.

2. Virtually everything in a publishing contract is negotiable.

3. If something *isn't* negotiable, your editor will clearly say so. Confirm this with a question such as, "You mean this can't be changed for any reason under any circumstances?" If the editor says, "That's right," believe it.

4. Before you begin negotiating any agreement, look it over carefully at least two or three times, noting every point and every word. Make a list of everything that you think needs changing. Then prioritize this list; note the things that you absolutely must have, the things you want but can live without, and the things that you'd like but don't seriously expect to get.

5. Stay calm, businesslike, and unemotional throughout all negotiations, no matter what your editor says—even if you're offered far more (or less) money, or far better (or worse) terms than you expected.

6. Different publishers and publications have different priorities in contract negotiation. One magazine may absolutely insist on buying one-time reprint rights as well as first serial rights; another may be happy with purchasing only one-time nonexclusive rights.

7. No editor will break a deal simply because you've asked for better terms. The worst that will happen is that you're told, "Either take my original offer or leave it"—and even this doesn't happen very often.

8. You are the one asking for changes in the contract, so you are the one who should control the negotiations. Be assertive. Lead your editor point by point through the contract, being clear and unhesitant about asking for what you want and need.

9. Once discussions begin, keep in mind those additions and changes you absolutely must have (if any), and remind yourself that you would rather pass up the deal than do without them. *If something is truly unacceptable, don't accept it.*

10. Be reasonable and flexible, but stick up for what's important to you. Push hard on the most important points; push less on small points, or let them go entirely.

11. The initial offer to publish your piece may be made by phone

or mail. You may then conduct negotiations in either manner (or both), as you choose.

12. You may negotiate the points in a contract in the order in which they appear in the document, or from the most to least important, as you prefer.

13. The stronger your credentials as writer are, the more you can ask for, and the more you are likely to get.

14. Don't be surprised if your editor — even a normally friendly and cooperative one — suddenly turns aggressive, impatient, gruff, intimidating, or even nasty when the time comes to negotiate a contract. Don't let this bother you; it is nothing more than a tactic. Ignore your editor's attitude and stick to the issues. Assume that the editor will return to normal once a deal has been struck.

15. Don't agree to anything prematurely. Once you've said yes, even if only verbally, that part of the negotiations is closed. If you need time to consider something, say so — and insist on taking it. Some writers insist on thinking over any deal overnight before coming to a decision. No editor will withdraw or worsen a deal because you have taken a day or two to consider it.

16. Push for clarity. Insist that any vague or ambiguous language be changed to language that is clear and unequivocal.

17. Be willing to negotiate individual words and phrases if necessary. Sometimes the change or addition of a single word, even a punctuation point, can make a big difference.

18. Never agree to anything you don't understand. If necessary, ask for advice from a literary attorney, agent, or writing consultant. Most will consult with writers on contract matters for an hourly fee. (Do *not* ask for advice from lawyers who do not specialize in literary matters; publishing contracts are Greek to them.) It is also possible to bring in an agent or literary attorney to negotiate on your behalf; see "19 Guidelines for Approaching Agents" on pages 158-160 for details.

19. If you're not happy with something as it's written, suggest specific language to replace it.

20. If your editor balks at a suggested change, explain why you want or need it. Similarly, if you object to a certain provision, ask your editor its purpose. Once you each understand the other's reasons, and know what the other

needs, it is often possible to write new language to accommodate both of you.

21. Here are some useful questions to ask in negotiations:
    a. What's the most you can offer? (Or, what's the best you can do?)
    b. You say you can't do such-and-such for me; have you ever done it for another writer? Why for them but not for me?
    c. Why is such-and-such a problem for you? What would solve that problem for you?
    d. What middle ground can we find on this issue?
    e. How about something in between what you and I have suggested?

22. Feel free to suggest alternatives, offer options, and propose compromises. These can all help enormously.

23. Offer tradeoffs. For example, if your editor absolutely refuses to increase your advance, say that you can live with it if the royalty rates are improved. The formula goes like this: "I'm willing to accept X if you'll let me have Y." Sometimes you can even get a large concession in exchange for a small one.

24. If your editor says no to a large change, suggest a smaller but similar change.

25. If you find something unacceptable, say so. Clearly state what would be acceptable in its place.

26. If you and your editor reach an impasse or get hung up on a point, suggest that you come back to it later. Once you've agreed on other points in the contract, you may find the sticky spots easier to deal with; or, with the rest of the agreement wrapped up, one or both of you may feel more inclined to give some ground.

27. Sometimes no means no; sometimes no means maybe. If you get a no, suggest a slightly different option, or ask, "Under what circumstances can you give me a yes on this?" If your editor responds to this with, "Sorry, I just can't do it," assume the answer really is no.

28. If you are told, "I'm sorry, but that's our policy," this doesn't always mean that the policy can't be bent a bit. If you feel you can, explain why your case merits a one-time exception to the policy. Or, ask your editor to ask their superior if the policy can be bent this one time for you.

(Don't try to get the policy itself changed; this almost never works.)

29. Negotiations on a book can often take quite a while, and can go on for several rounds. Be patient and let them take as long as they have to. Don't let your impatience make you agree to something you'll regret later.

30. You don't always have to negotiate a publishing contract. If what you're offered looks fine (and it will about 40 percent of the time for short work), accept the terms as they are. Every book contract, however, will require at least some negotiation.

31. Carefully reread *every copy* of your contract after any changes have been made in it. *Do not trust publishers or agents to make all changes correctly*, because they simply won't.

32. If you have an agent, do not leave contract negotiations entirely up to them. Once you receive a copy of your contract, look it over *extremely* carefully. If you need or want additional changes, tell your agent what they are and insist that they be pursued.

33. If you cannot come to terms and back out of a deal, then later decide that you can live with those terms, there is nothing wrong with getting back to the editor and saying, "I think we can strike a deal after all." However, the editor has the right to respond with, "Sorry; it's too late."

34. See "24 Tips on Asking for More Money" on pages 123-125 for negotiating strategies specifically related to money.

35. For a more extended discussion on negotiating publishing agreements, consult one or more of these books:
    a. *A Writer's Guide to Contract Negotiations* by Richard Balkin (Writer's Digest Books)
    b. *Negotiating a Book Contract* by Mark L. Levine (Moyer Bell)
    c. *The Indispensable Writer's Guide* by Scott Edelstein (HarperCollins)

    Another excellent book on negotiation in general is *Getting to Yes* by Roger Fisher and William Uri (Houghton Mifflin; Penguin).

Altering a Written Agreement

1. The great majority of publishers and producers have no objection to your making changes in a written agreement. A few book publishers, though, insist that after negotiations are complete, you return the unamended contracts to them. These publishers then amend the contracts themselves and return them to you for your final approval and signing. When dealing with book publishers, ask to make sure that you may make written changes.
2. Before making any changes, make a photocopy of the unaltered contract. If you make an uncorrectable error on the original, simply remove that page and use a photocopy of it instead.
3. Make all changes clearly, neatly, and readably.
4. Use black indelible pen for small changes. Type in additions and changes of more than a few words, when possible.
5. To omit any words or line, simply draw a single clear line through it. If you need to omit an entire section or paragraph, do this for every line.
6. To make a change, draw a line through the material you wish to omit; add the replacement language in its place.
7. To add material, add a carat ($\wedge$) in the appropriate spot and write or type in the addition immediately above.
8. When space does not permit using a carat to insert material, insert just an asterisk instead. Elsewhere on the same page (either in the margin to the immediate left or right of the paragraph, or at the bottom of the page), type the asterisk again, immediately followed by the language you wish to add (just as you would present a footnote).
9. To avoid confusion, use a different symbol for each footnoted addition in your contract. Use an asterisk for the first; use a different nonnumerical symbol (@, #, $, %, etc.) for each of the others.
10. If even a footnote will be too long to fit on the page, write or type "See rider" after the symbol in the margin or at the

bottom. At the end of the entire contract, type the heading "Rider to paragraph _____:," followed by the language you wish to insert. Attach an additional page for riders if necessary.

11. All of the following are acceptable:
    a. Making changes and additions in mid-sentence.
    b. Making several changes in the same sentence.
    c. Changing or omitting individual letters or punctuation points. (Usually this is done to add clarity or eliminate ambiguity.)
    d. Adding or deleting whole paragraphs and sections. New paragraphs and sections are usually added at the end of the document as numbered items (e.g., Paragraph 14).

12. Initial each of your changes, omissions, and additions, including all riders. Before you return the signed contracts, double-check that you have put your initials in every necessary spot. These changes must also be initialed by someone at your publisher or production company to be valid.

13. Sign and date all copies of your agreement; add your social security number if it is requested. If a witness's signature is required, obtain it.

14. Your agreement is complete when you and your publisher or producer each have a copy of the final amended contract, with both signatures and both sets of initials on each change. Once you receive a copy of the completed agreement, check it to make sure that the other party has signed it and initialed every change; if they haven't, send it back and request the additions.

15. A very few periodical publishers print contracts on the backs of checks; cashing or depositing the check constitutes agreement to the printed terms. If you are not happy with the terms, change them as necessary according to the guidelines above (and according to any terms you may have previously agreed to covering the use of your piece); then sign and deposit (or cash) the check.

Making an Oral Contract

1. A clear oral agreement is a serious commitment, and is legally binding.

2. Expect and be willing to make oral contracts:
   a. With newspapers (except a few of the largest big-city dailies).
   b. With newsletters.
   c. With very small magazines (particularly those that pay writers little or nothing).
   d. In circumstances where you expect to make little or no money (e.g., the production of your play at a community center).
3. Do not make an oral contract for any of the following:
   a. Publication of a book.
   b. Newspaper or magazine syndication.
   c. *Major* production of material for stage, film, TV, audio, or audiovisual media.
   d. Publication of any other self-contained material (e.g., computer software).
   Insist upon a written agreement for any of the above.
4. If the other party does not bring up a certain point for negotiation or agreement, do so yourself.
5. Be clear, explicit, and unambiguous about all the terms of your contract, and about the fact that you agree to those terms.
6. As you discuss each of the terms, write down all the details.
7. Once you've talked over all the terms one by one, say, "Let me go through my list with you to make sure I've got everything right." Then quickly read through your entire list aloud to confirm your contract.
8. It is often a good idea to follow up your oral agreement with a short letter to your editor. Outline the terms you've agreed upon, and say something like, "This is my understanding of what we've agreed to. If your understanding is different, let me know." This adds extra protection to your contract. (This step is not necessary for deals with very small publications such as neighborhood newspapers.)
9. In the absence of any contract at all, either oral or written, beyond "you can use my piece" (and perhaps "we'll pay you $_____"), then, under U.S. law, the following terms apply: you have given the publication the right to print your piece *in that publication only* as many times as your editor pleases—which, in practice, is almost always only once.

Determining Which Rights to Sell

1. Publishers and producers typically try to buy as many rights as they can; as a general rule, writers should try to give up as few rights as possible. This enables them to sell those rights separately, and make more money.
2. Rights are almost always negotiable — even when you are told "we buy such-and-such rights," "these are our standard terms," or "this is our regular contract." There's nothing wrong with being an exception or asking for something different.
3. Never sell all rights to a piece in exchange for a single flat fee; insist on either limiting the rights sold (to first worldwide periodical rights, worldwide English-language rights, etc.) and/or to getting a percentage of whatever money the piece earns (e.g., a per-copy royalty, a percentage of money earned from the sale of subsidiary rights, etc.). One exception: sell all rights for a flat fee if that fee is enormous.
4. When selling a piece to a magazine, newspaper, or newsletter, normally sell first North American serial rights only. (A serial is the same as a periodical: a newspaper, newsletter, or magazine.) Exceptions:
   a. If the periodical is published both in and outside of North America, agree to sell the right to publish your piece for the first time throughout the world in that periodical only (or, if the editor insists, in periodicals published by that company only). If you absolutely must, agree to first worldwide serial rights in general.
   b. If a periodical wants to buy reprint as well as first rights, be willing to grant them on a nonexclusive basis only. Insist that you be paid a separate fee for each reprint use. Specify the following: when the publisher reprints the piece in one of its own publications, the fee shall be at least 25 percent of the fee paid for first publication; when reprint rights are sold to another publisher, you shall be paid at least 50 percent of all money received by the publisher, within thirty days of receipt.
   c. Some Canadian periodicals are not sold or distributed outside of Canada. When dealing with these publications, normally sell first Canadian serial rights only.

d. If a periodical wishes to buy one-time nonexclusive use instead of first serial rights, this is fine.

e. If the periodical is published only outside of North America, try to sell only first serial rights in that language or territory (e.g., first German-language serial rights, first Japanese serial rights, first British Commonwealth serial rights, etc.) or one-time nonexclusive rights in that language or territory.

5. Always sell reprint rights on a one-time, nonexclusive basis. This means that the publisher can publish your piece only once, and that you can continue to sell reprint rights to other publishers in the same territory or language. (Foreign rights are sometimes an exception; see items 4e above and 7 below.)

6. When selling the right to use your piece in an anthology, insist on one of the following sets of terms:

   a. You grant the right to use your piece in all editions of the anthology worldwide; you receive a negotiated fee on the signing of your contract, which covers the initial edition only. You shall be paid an additional fee on the publication of each reprint edition; this fee shall not be less than 40 percent (or 30 percent, or 25 percent — but no less) of your initial fee.

   b. You grant the right to use your piece in all editions of the anthology worldwide; you receive a negotiated fee on the signing of your contract, which covers the initial edition only. You shall be paid a **pro-rated** share of 60 percent (or 50 percent — but no less) of all the money the anthology editor receives for all future editions. (Pro-rated means all contributors share the money, based on the percentage of pieces, pages, or words they have contributed to the book.)

   c. You grant the right to use your piece in all editions of the anthology worldwide; you receive a negotiated fee on the signing of your contract. You shall also be paid a pro-rated share of 60 percent (or 50 percent — but no less) of all the money the anthology editor earns from the book beyond its initial advance, including royalties on the initial edition.

   d. You grant the right to use your piece in the first edition of the anthology only; inclusion in later editions shall be separately negotiated. (Recommended only for big-name authors.)

e. Same as a, b, c, or d above, but without the payment of an initial fee. (Agree to this only in the case of a scholarly or professional book—and then only after you have asked for an initial fee and been told no.)

f. Same as a, b, c, or d above, but without any payment at any time. (Agree to this only for scholarly books.)

Items a and c are ideal; b is not quite as good, but still fair. Under no circumstances permit anthology use of your work without a clear written agreement.

7. If you are selling your book, try to sell North American publication rights only, and try to hang onto television, film, audio, video, and dramatic rights. [If the publisher is not based in North America, try to limit the rights you sell to the appropriate language or territory—e.g., the British Commonwealth (excluding Canada), France, Italy, etc.] Also insist on at least a 50/50 split on all money from subsidiary rights sales. Most publishers will accept the 50/50 split but will want to control more rights.

8. If a book publisher must have more rights, here are some you might give up:

a. Foreign/translation rights (ask for 75 percent of all such money, which is standard; accept 65 percent, 60 percent, or 50 percent only if the publisher insists; refuse anything less than 50 percent).

b. British Commonwealth rights (percentages same as above).

c. Worldwide English language rights (percentages same as above for all subsidiary rights sales).

d. TV, film, audio, video, and/or dramatic rights (ask for 90 percent of this money, which is standard; accept 75 percent if absolutely necessary).

9. If a book publisher wants to buy all rights, normally you should say no. However, if you do not have an agent, or if your agent does not handle foreign rights, it may be a good idea to sell all rights so that your publisher can act as your agent in selling foreign and other subsidiary rights. Insist upon your fair share of money from such sales, of course.

10. Strange as it sounds, in publishing, North American rights normally include the United States, Canada, Guam, Puerto

Rico, the U.S. Virgin Islands, the Philippines, and a few other tiny territories. Don't try to exclude any of these countries in your negotiating; you'll simply be told no.

11. Newspapers and newsletters normally buy one-time North American serial rights only. In the absence of a specific oral or written agreement, assume that these are the terms. In the absence of such an agreement with a magazine, however, *make* a clear agreement.

12. Some magazines and anthologies may wish to buy all rights, but will agree in their contracts to return all but first serial rights to you on publication (or shortly thereafter), either automatically or on your written request. This is to keep you from selling reprint rights to your piece until after it has been published. Agree to this if you are asked to, but insist on the following provisions as well:

   a. You may begin selling reprint rights no later than three months after publication.

   b. All rights revert to you if your piece is not published within one year (eighteen months, if your editor insists, but no more).

Marketing Subsidiary and Foreign Rights

1. Once you have sold first rights to a piece, you are free to immediately market any reprint and/or foreign rights that you have retained (unless your contract specifically prohibits you from doing so).

2. You may try to sell any and all types of subsidiary rights simultaneously.

3. Because most subsidiary rights are sold on a nonexclusive basis, you may sell the same piece over and over. There are two general limitations:

   a. You may not sell reprint rights to a piece to publications that have significantly overlapping audiences.

   b. You may not sell television or film rights (or an option on such rights) to more than one producer at a time.

4. If the initial publisher of your piece has not purchased rights in a particular language or territory — say, French — then you may sell first French-language serial rights to a French-language publication. This will usually entitle you to more money than one-time nonexclusive French-language use.

5. When approaching editors in foreign countries, write your cover letter and all subsequent correspondence in English, unless you are fluent in the appropriate language.
6. If your piece has already been published, submit photocopies of the appropriate pages from the periodical or anthology rather than a manuscript (unless you wish to submit a rewritten or other alternate version). In the case of books, you may submit galleys, page proofs, a copy of the published book, or, if you prefer, a manuscript copy.
7. Some North American agents have a network of foreign agents (called subagents) who handle foreign rights in their own countries and languages; some agents, however, have few or no such contacts. If you have an agent, feel free to seek representation in any country or language in which there is no affiliated subagent; if you have no agent at all, seek representation in any foreign country you wish.

Collecting Overdue Payments

Always keep careful records of when any funds and/or royalty statements are due you. If you have not received what you are owed by the due date, follow these guidelines:

Collecting From Publishers and Producers
1. Wait ten business days beyond the due date. Then call your editor (or your other regular contact at that organization). Explain the problem and ask — politely, calmly, and firmly — that your contact look into it, take care of it, *and get back to you on it*. If you are referred to someone else within the organization, make these requests of this person.
2. Give this person one week to get back to you with information; if they don't, call again. If they do not take or return your call, try again a few days later; if the second call is not returned, skip to step 4 below.
3. If you are told that you will be paid shortly, wait three to four more weeks. If after this time you still have not been paid, go to step 4.
4. Write a letter to the head of the organization (if you don't know their name, call to find out). Explain the situation in language that is terse, firm, straightforward, and

businesslike—but not accusatory, demanding, or threatening. End your letter with language such as this: "I trust you will resolve this problem for both of us quickly. Please call if you have any questions." Send this letter by certified or registered mail, return receipt requested. Also send photocopies of the letter via regular mail to your editor (or other regular contact) and anyone else you might have dealt with regarding the problem (such as the accounting department).

5. If you are not paid within thirty days, call the head of the organization. If they take your call, briefly explain the situation again and insist on being paid within fifteen business days. Be firm and insistent, but not angry. If they do not take or return your call, try again a few days later. Either way, if you are not paid within fifteen business days, go to step 6.

6. The organization has no intention of paying you, so do one of the following:
   a. Forget about it.
   b. Go to an attorney. Spend about $50 to have them call or write the head honcho who has been ignoring you. About half the time this will do the trick.

7. If you have still not been paid one month after your lawyer has called or written, you have three options left:
   a. File a lawsuit. (For sums of a few thousand dollars or less, the case can usually be tried in small claims court; this costs very little and does not require an attorney.)
   b. Contact an arbitrator, in the (slim) hope that the problem can be solved through arbitration.
   c. Give up.

8. Do not alter your approach if you are told that the organization is cash-poor, or having a cash-flow problem, or going through a financial crisis. *This does not alter its obligation to you.* The one exception is if you are formally informed that the organization has filed for reorganization or bankruptcy, in which case its debt to you is put on hold indefinitely.

9. Throughout the entire process, let your editor or other regular contact know what is going on, and keep asking them to do what they can to see to it that you are paid.

Collecting From Clients for Whom You Have Provided Services

1. If you have not been paid by the due date on your invoice, send a second invoice, identical to the first, with these exceptions:
   a. Place the current date at the top.
   b. Two lines below the date, type in all capitals or bold face: "Second Notice—Past Due Amount."
   c. If you have received partial payment, indicate this as a credit and adjust the total amount due accordingly.
2. Wait one more month. If you have not received payment in full by this time, call your regular contact within the organization (usually the person you reported to or did the work for) to discuss the problem. Ask—politely, calmly, and firmly—that they look into it, take care of it, *and get back to you on it.* If they refer you to someone else within the organization (usually someone in bookkeeping), make these requests of this person.
3. Give this person one week to get back to you with information; if they don't, call again. If they do not take or return your call, try again a few days later; if they do not take or return this second call, skip to step 5 below.
4. If you are told that you will be paid shortly, wait three to four more weeks. If after this time you still have not been paid, go to step 5.
5. Follow steps 4 through 9 from "Collecting From Publishers and Producers" as necessary.

28 Basics of Copyright You Should Know

1. **Rights** are different from **copyright**. As soon as you create something, you own all rights to it, and may keep, sell, or give away any or all of those rights as you please. **Copyright** refers to legal protection from unauthorized publication or production of your work provided by the federal government. It is possible to own the copyright to a piece, but few or no rights to it; it is also possible to control most or all of the rights to a piece, but not hold the copyright.
2. Copyright law covers publication and most forms of public performance and display. Books, articles, stories, essays, songs, poems, scripts of all types, records, audio tapes, videotapes, photographs, works of visual art, and virtually

all other creative endeavors receive copyright protection.

3. *Your piece is legally protected and fully copyrighted from the moment you create it.* You do not need to formally register a piece with the copyright office until it is published or performed before an audience. At that time, however, it must be registered in order for copyright protection to continue.

4. Copyright protection begins as soon as a work exists in some physical form. Ideas, extemporaneous speeches, conversations, and other items not in tangible form are not protected. However, once those same ideas, speeches, conversations, or other items are recorded in some way — on tape, on record, on paper, etc. — they immediately receive full copyright protection.

5. Copyright protection begins the moment a work is created and continues until:

   In the United States: copyright protection extends until the end of the fiftieth full calendar year after the year in which the author dies.

   In Canada: copyright protection extends until the fiftieth anniversary of the author's death.

   In either case, protection continues for this period whether or not the work has been published or performed — provided that, if it *is* published or performed, it is (or has previously been) properly registered with the copyright office. There are a few exceptions to these general rules, however:

   a. For collaborative works, U.S. copyright protection extends until the end of the fiftieth full calendar year after the year of death of the last surviving coauthor. In Canada, protection continues until the fiftieth anniversary of the death of the last surviving coauthor.

   b. Copyright coverage for pseudonymous works is identical to coverage for works published under the authors' own names, with one exception. In the U.S. only, if an author chooses to copyright a work in their pen name *and* withholds their real name from the U.S. copyright office, then copyright protection extends until the end of the seventy-fifth full calendar year following the piece's initial U.S. publication or performance, *or* the end of the hundredth full calendar year following the year of its creation, whichever comes first. In Canada, this option is not available; all authors *must* provide the copyright office with their real names. In either country, you may copyright a pseudonymous work in either your real name or your pen name, as you prefer.

   c. If a work is copyrighted in the name of a magazine, publishing firm, or other business or organization, all of the rules above continue to apply, with the copyright for any piece normally extending for fifty years after the death of the author, regardless of whose name the copyright is in. In the case of a magazine or anthology, each piece included as part of that publication receives its own separate copyright protection—again, normally until fifty years after the author's death. The anthology or magazine issue *also* receives its own copyright protection as a collective work.

   d. Copyrights may not be renewed, except on works published in the United States before 1978. For details on pre-1978 U.S. copyright law, call the U.S. Copyright Office (202-707-3000). Canadian copyrights are non-renewable.

   e. In Canada, copyright coverage for records, tapes, photographs, certain other non-print media, and posthumously-published works is slightly different from the coverage for written works described above.

6. You do not need to mail your work to yourself to initiate copyright protection. Simply save a copy of each manuscript you write, plus a copy of one early draft as evidence that you created the piece. In practice, it is exceedingly unlikely that your authorship of any piece will ever be challenged.

7. Copyright protection cannot actually prevent people from using your work without your permission, any more than a law against theft can completely eliminate stealing. However, if your work is used without your permission, you can sue for both compensation and damages, and the law is on your side.

8. You may register any of your unpublished works (or any group of your unpublished and/or published works under a single title) with the copyright office at any time. This is not necessary at all, but many writers do it entirely for their own piece of mind. For registration information, see item 16 below. If you register an unpublished work, it does not

need to be reregistered when it is first published—unless it is published in significantly different form.

9. When one of your pieces is published in a copyrighted newspaper, magazine, or anthology, copyright protection is simultaneously extended to your piece as an individual work and to the entire book or periodical in which your piece appears. This holds true whether or not your piece has been previously published.

10. Physical possession of a manuscript in no way affects ownership of either rights or copyright to it.

11. The great majority of book publishers will copyright your work for you in your name (or, if your prefer, in your pseudonym) on publication at no charge. Make sure your publication contract guarantees this. Exception: textbooks are often copyrighted in the publisher's name. However, if you've written a textbook, it is worth at least asking to have your book copyrighted in your own name.

12. Publishers of magazines and newspapers normally copyright each issue and edition in their own name. Copyright protection then automatically extends to every piece in that issue or edition.

13. Film and television production companies almost invariably copyright scripts in their own names.

14. If your play is about to be produced for the first time, check with the producing organization to make sure that it registers the play with the copyright office, and does so in your name. If it doesn't, register it yourself.

15. If you self-publish one of your own books, register it with the copyright office as soon as possible after publication. Order the appropriate forms about two months in advance.

16. To register your work with the copyright office, write or call one of the following:
    a. In the United States:
       Write: Copyright Office, Library of Congress, Washington, D.C. 20559.
       Or call: 202-707-3000 (for general information, and to determine which form(s) you will need); 202-707-9100 (to request specific forms).
    b. In Canada:
       Write: Copyright and Industrial Design Branch, 50 Victoria Street, Place du Portage, Tower 1, Hull, QUE

K1A 0C9.
Or call: 613-997-1725.
Once you have registered a piece with the copyright office, you will receive a certificate of copyright for it. Save this certificate indefinitely.

17. When a piece is published in any form, it must be accompanied by a proper copyright notice. An example of a proper copyright notice appears at the beginning of this book. Guidelines on printing such a notice are provided with copyright registration forms.

18. When a collection of your previously-published work is published, it must be reregistered as a separate work.

19. Titles cannot be copyrighted. This means that you may use any title you choose, even if someone else has used it before. It also means that anyone else is free to use any title you decide on. Your characters, however, belong to you; no one else may use them in their own work without your explicit permission.

20. Names, catchphrases, and lists of ingredients cannot be copyrighted. Promotional slogans and product names cannot be copyrighted either, but they usually can be trademarked.

21. There is only one situation where copyright protection does not extend to you as soon as you write a piece. If you work for someone else, any writing you do *as part of your regular job* becomes the property of your employer as soon as it is created, and copyright protection is immediately extended to your employer, not to you.

22. Once copyright protection on a piece has expired, that piece is in the **public domain**. This means that anyone can publish or perform it anywhere at any time without first securing permission, so long as the author is given a proper byline. Works published but not registered with the copyright office are also considered to be in the public domain until they are registered.

23. Although in general no one may publish, produce, or reproduce any of your work without your permission (unless it is in the public domain), very brief excerpts *may* be used without your permission under what is called **fair use** in the U.S. or **fair dealing** in Canada. These excerpts must not represent a significant portion of your piece; in

practice, 200 to 300 words of prose and 1 to 2 lines of poetry are the normal limits. Anyone wishing to use longer excerpts must request your permission to do so.

24. A separate copyright must normally be obtained for each country in which a piece is published. Most countries comply with a series of uniform international copyright standards.

25. Pieces first published or performed in the United States before 1978 are affected by different copyright rules; call the U.S. Copyright Office (202-707-3000) for details.

26. It is not necessary, appropriate, or advisable to place a copyright notice on any manuscript you submit to an editor, agent, or producer. If the piece has been previously published, simply say where and when in your cover letter.

27. Both the United States and Canadian copyright offices publish helpful copyright guides which are free on request:
    a. In the United States:
       Circular 1: *Copyright Basics*
       Circular 2: *Copyright Publications*
       To order, write the Information and Publications Section, LM-455, Copyright Office, Library of Congress, Washington, D.C. 20559, or call 202-707-9100.
    b. In Canada:
       Copyright Questions and Answers
       To order, write the Copyright and Industrial Design Branch, 50 Victoria Street, Place du Portage, Tower 1, Hull, QUE K1A 0C9, or call 613-997-1725.

28. For detailed information on U.S. copyright laws, consult one or more of these books:
    a. *Every Writer's Guide to Copyright and Publishing Law* by Ellen M. Kozak (Holt). This is the best book on the subject.
    b. *How to Protect Your Creative Work* by David A. Weinstein (Wiley)
    c. *A Writer's Guide to Copyright* by Caroline R. Herron (Poets & Writers, Inc.)

Averting Literary Theft

1. Your work is fully protected under copyright law from the time you create it. You do not need to copyright it yourself, file any forms, store a copy in a safe deposit box, or mail a copy to yourself. Simply keep a copy of each finished manuscript (and, if you like, of one prior draft as well) in your files.
2. Do not include a copyright notice on any manuscript or in any cover letter. However, if you are submitting a previously published piece, state in your cover letter where and when the piece was first published. When you do sell reprint rights, supply your editor with a proper copyright notice (e.g., Copyright 1991 by F&W Publications), and request that it be run with your piece.
3. Remember that nothing you do can absolutely prevent someone from stealing your work or ideas, any more than prison or death sentences can completely prevent murder. You can, however, sue anyone who has improperly used your material, and chances are you'll win.
4. In general, copyright law protects your words, characters, and plots. It does *not* protect individual ideas or titles, which are entirely up for grabs. Thus, anyone may legally call their novel *Gone with the Wind*, but they may not publish a piece using another writer's characters without that writer's permission.
5. You need not fear that someone else will publish your work under their own name. This virtually never happens in print publishing and theatre, and occurs only rarely in TV and film.
6. By far the most common type of literary theft involves reprinting a previously published work under the author's proper byline, but without first acquiring the permission of the author or the initial publisher. If this happens to you, do the following:
   a. Write a letter to the head of the organization (usually whomever has the title of publisher) by name.
   b. In your letter, let this person know that you're aware of the unauthorized use of your piece. Include all appropriate titles and dates.
   c. Explain politely but firmly that this is a violation of both

copyright law and standard publishing practices.

    d. Offer to grant retroactive permission to use your piece in exchange for a fee to be paid within thirty days. Specify a fee that is between 150 to 200 percent of what you would expect that publication to normally pay to use that piece. If the publication is very small and looks like it normally pays little or nothing for material, ask for $100-$300.

    e. Close your letter with a sentence such as, "I hope and expect you will settle this matter promptly."

    f. Send this letter by certified or registered mail, return receipt requested. Save the proof of delivery notice.

    g. If after six weeks you have not received the amount you have specified, either let the matter drop or take the publisher to arbitration or court. (Few such cases do actually go to court; those that do usually go to small claims court.)

7. If you have written something for television or film, it is an excellent idea to register it with the Writers Guild (in the United States) or the Alliance of Canadian Cinema, Television, and Radio Artists (in Canada). This provides additional protection against theft. Contact The Writers Guild West, 7000 West 3rd Street, Los Angeles, CA 90048, 213-951-4000, or The Writers Guild East, 555 West 57th Street, Suite 1230, New York, NY 10019, 212-757-4360; or, in Canada, ACCTRA, 2239 Yonge Street, 3rd floor, Toronto, ONT M4S 2B5. 416-489-1311. Registration is not necessary or recommended for audio or radio scripts.

Using a Pen Name

1. You may use one or more pen names (or **pseudonyms**) whenever you wish, for any reason you wish, with these exceptions:

    a. You may not use a pen name already being used by someone else.

    b. You may not use the name of a real person known to you (e.g., Barbara Bush or Scott Edelstein). However,

Barbara Busch and S.M. Edelstein are kosher. (So are names of everyday folks—e.g., Mary Williams—so long as you know no one by that name yourself.)

    c. You may not use the name of a fictional character from another writer's work (such as Winston Smith or Wilma Flintstone) without that writer's permission.

    d. You may not use a name that is obscene or libelous.

2. Keep in mind these common reasons why people use pen names:

    a. To disassociate themselves from something they've written—an exposé, erotica, a trashy romance novel, etc.

    b. To limit or avoid publicity and public attention.

    c. To keep their personal and literary lives separate.

    d. To keep from spoiling their reputations (as a minister, trusted employee, exemplary member of the community, etc.). Academics who write popular fiction often use a pseudonym on their fiction to protect their scholarly reputations.

    e. Their real name is ugly, hard to spell or pronounce or remember, too long, too similar or identical to someone else's (e.g., Barbara Bush), silly-sounding, or highly inappropriate (e.g., they've written a romance novel and their name is Ed Schmertz).

    f. To establish a separate literary identity (and perhaps a separate literary persona).

    g. To build careers in two or more different fields of writing, with a different name for material in each field. (Usually, but not always, one of these names is their real one.)

3. In the following cases, you may be required to adopt a pen name:

    a. You have written a genre novel (particularly a romance novel or male adventure) and your normal byline doesn't suit the genre.

    b. You've written a novel in a series that uses a "house name"—a single pseudonym that the publisher uses for all books in the series.

    c. Your own name is very long, silly, or odd.

    d. Your work reveals information that could result in harm

to you were your real identity known.

e. Your employer (e.g., the CIA) requires that you not publish anything under your own name.

4. In general, pick a pseudonym that is fairly easy to spell and remember, that is not easily confused with the name of another writer or personality, and that is not inappropriate for your material.

5. It is fair game for women to use masculine pen names and for men to use feminine ones.

6. You do not need to (and, indeed, cannot) register, patent, or copyright a pseudonym.

7. Each of your pieces may be copyrighted in either your pen name or your own name, as you choose.

8. Normally you should use your real name in all your dealings with publishers and producers, who will automatically keep your identity concealed from others. However, if you wish, you may conceal your identity from everyone but your agent. Tell your agent that you wish your identity kept completely secret; on your manuscripts, list your pseudonym as both the byline and the author's name.

9. Except as noted above, place your own name just above your address on all manuscripts; use your pseudonym only as your byline. For poetry manuscripts of less than book-length, omit your pseudonym entirely; mention it to your editor only after your work has been accepted (or, if you have already established a reputation under your pen name, in your cover letter).

10. Publishers, producers, and agents will normally make out checks to your real name unless you specifically request otherwise. If you do wish checks to be made out to your pseudonym, arrange with your bank in advance for it to accept these payments as deposits to your account. Or, if you prefer, open an AKA (also known as) account.

6 Tips on Collaboration

1. There are as many ways to collaborate as there are pieces that can be jointly written. You and your coauthor can work together on every sentence; one can do the research and the other the writing; the two (or more) of you can alternate sections, scenes, or chapters; one can do a first draft and

another the rewriting and polishing; or you can work out some other arrangement that works for both (or all) of you.

2. There are usually some disagreements even in the best of collaborations. Remember that negotiation and compromise are usually more productive than fighting or scuttling the project. Collaboration is a business relationship, and both (or all) of you share a single goal: completing the writing project satisfactorily.

3. Before you or your coauthor(s) do any significant amount of work on your project, you must come to some agreement on the following issues:

   a. How will earnings from the project be divided? (Typically, income is divided equally among all collaborators.)

   b. How will the work be divided? This includes researching, writing, typing, and submitting a final manuscript.

   c. Who will give interviews, make appearances on talk shows, give readings, or otherwise promote the project? How will the money resulting from these efforts be divided?

   d. How will any expenses involved in the writing, research, submission, and promotion of the project be divided?

   e. How will any other potential expenses, both expected (such as manuscript typing and illustrations) and unexpected (legal fees, etc.) be split? If you are publishing the project yourselves, how will publication and advertising costs be divided?

   f. Whose agent will represent the project?

   g. How will the various "chores" be divided? Who will handle correspondence regarding the project? Who will proofread the final manuscript, correct galleys, prepare the index, etc.?

   h. Will one coauthor receive all payments, then distribute the money to other collaborators within ten days? If so, who? Or will publishers and/or agents be instructed to write a separate check to each coauthor?

   i. What will be done in the event of a disagreement? (Many collaborators decide in advance to turn over any unresolvable disagreements to a mutually acceptable arbitrator, whose decision will be legally binding.)

4. Before you do much writing, draw up a *written* agreement covering all of the appropriate points above. Make sure all coauthors have signed and dated this agreement; keep a copy of it in your files.
5. If for some reason you must scuttle a project, make a clear agreement about who retains the right to complete it, either alone or in collaboration with someone else.
6. Some collaborations are not really collaborations at all. If you are writing a worthwhile project but have few or no credentials (either in publishing or in the subject you're writing on), it is perfectly kosher to forge a mock collaboration with someone who does have the correct credentials or whose name is well known. Under such an arrangement, you do all (or the great majority) of the writing, but share the byline with someone whose name lends authority and/or appeal to the project. In such an arrangement it remains essential to follow steps 3 and 4 above.

More Great
Books for Writers!

How to Write a Book Proposal, Revised Edition—Get your nonfiction published as you learn the basics of creating effective book proposals with experienced literary agent, Michael Larsen. From test marketing potential book ideas to creating a professional-looking proposal package, you'll cover every step that's essential for breaking into the publishing market! *#10518/$14.99/224 pages/paperback*

Building Fiction: How to Develop Plot & Structure—Even with the most dynamic language, images and characters, no piece of fiction will work without a strong infrastructure. This book shows you how to build that structure using such tools as point of view, characterization, pacing, conflict, and transitional devices such as flashbacks. With Jesse Lee Kercheval's guidance, you will build a work of fiction just as an architect would design a house—with an eye for details and how all the parts of a story or novel interconnect. *#48028/$16.99/208 pages/paperback*

Writing the Private Eye Novel: A Handbook by the Private Eye Writers of America—Discover pages of advice on writing and publishing PI novels—from authors whose fiction flys off the shelves. You'll find 23 tip-filled chapters on topics that include plot structure, character development, setting and short stories. Plus, specific advice on finding ideas, keeping readers on edge, creating slam-bang endings and more! *#10519/$18.99/240 pages*

Grammatically Correct: The Writer's Guide to Punctuation, Spelling, Style, Usage and Grammar—Write prose that's clear, concise and graceful! This comprehensive desk reference covers the nuts-and-bolts basics of punctuation, spelling and grammar, as well as essential tips and techniques for developing a smooth, inviting writing style. *#10529/$19.99/352 pages*

Elements of the Writing Craft—Apply the techniques of the masters in your own work! This collection of 150 lessons reveals how noted writers have "built" their fiction and nonfiction. Each exercise contains a short passage of work from a distinguished writer, a writer's-eye analysis of the passage and a wealth of innovative writing exercises. *#48027/$19.99/272 pages*

Writer's Digest Handbook of Making Money Freelance Writing—Discover promising new income-producing opportunities with this collection of articles by top writers, editors and agents. Over 30 commentaries on business issues, writing opportunities and freelancing will help you make the break to a full-time writing career. *#10501/$19.99/320 pages*

The Writer's Digest Dictionary of Concise Writing—Make your work leaner, crisper and clearer! Under the guidance of professional editor Robert Hartwell Fiske, you'll learn how to rid your work of common say-nothing phrases while making it tighter and easier to read and understand. *#10482/$19.99/352 pages*

How to Write Attention-Grabbing Query & Cover Letters—Use the secrets John Wood reveals to write queries perfectly tailored, too good to turn down! In this guidebook, you will discover why boldness beats blandness in queries every time, ten basics you must have in your article queries, ten query blunders that can destroy publication chances and much more. *#10462/$17.99/208 pages*

The 30-Minute Writer—Write short, snappy articles that make editors sit up and take notice. Full-time freelancer Connie Emerson reveals the many types of quickly written articles you can sell—from miniprofiles and one-pagers to personal essays. You'll also learn how to match your work to the market as you explore methods for expanding from short articles to columns and even books! *#10489/$14.99/256 pages/paperback*

Writing to Sell, Fourth Edition—You'll discover high-quality writing and marketing counsel in this classic writing guide from well-known agent Scott Meredith. His timeless advice will guide you along the professional writing path as you get help with creating characters, plotting a novel, placing your work, formatting a manuscript, deciphering a publishing contract—even combating a slump! *#10476/$17.99/240 pages*

Writer's Encyclopedia, Third Edition—Rediscover this popular writer's reference—now with information about electronic resources, plus more than 100 new entries. You'll find facts, figures, definitions and examples designed to answer questions about every discipline connected with writing and help you convey a professional image. *#10464/$22.99/560 pages/62 b&w illus.*

Writing and Selling Your Novel—Write publishable fiction from start to finish with expert advice from professional novelist Jack Bickham! You'll learn how to develop effective work habits, refine your fiction writing technique, and revise and tailor your novels for tightly targeted markets. *#10509/$17.99/208 pages*

The Writer's Digest Handbook of Short Story Writing, Volume II—Orson Scott Card, Dwight V. Swain, Kit Reed and other noted authors bring you sound advice and timeless techniques for every aspect of the writing process. *#10239/$13.99/252 pages/paperback*

The Writer's Legal Guide, Revised Edition—Now the answer to all your legal questions is right at your fingertips! The updated version of this treasured desktop companion contains essential information on business issues, copyright protection and registration, contract negotiation, income taxation, electronic rights and much, much more. *#10478/$19.95/256 pages/paperback*

The Writer's Digest Sourcebook for Building Believable Characters—Create unforgettable characters as you "attend" a roundtable where six novelists reveal their approaches to characterization. You'll probe your characters' backgrounds, beliefs and desires with a fill-in-the-blanks questionnaire. And a thesaurus of characteristics will help you develop the many other features no character should be without. *#10463/$17.99/288 pages*

Get That Novel Written: From Initial Idea to Final Edit—Take your novel from the starting line to a fabulous finish! Professional writer Donna Levin shows you both the basics and the finer points of novel writing while you learn to use words with precision, create juicy conflicts, master point of view and more! *#10481/$18.99/208 pages*

Travel Writing: A Guide to Research, Writing and Selling—Bring your travels home in print as you discover the many types of articles there are to write—and how to do it. You'll learn how to make your journey into a salable article by finding information, verifying it and bringing it to life on paper. *#10465/$18.99/256 pages*

Romance Writer's Sourcebook: Where to Sell Your Manuscripts—Get your romance manuscripts published with this new resource guide that combines how-to-write instruction with where-to-sell direction. You'll uncover advice from established authors, as well as detailed listings of publishing houses, agents, organizations, contests and more! *#10456/$19.99/475 pages*